ACTION PHILOSOPHERS

Fred Van Lente & Ryan Dunlavey

 ™ Rocketship Entertainment, LLC
rocketshipent.com

Tom Akel, CEO & Publisher • **Rob Feldman,** CTO • **Jeanmarie McNeely,** CFO
Brandon Freeberg, Dir. of Campaign Mgmt. • **Phil Smith,** Art Director • **Aram Alekyan,** Designer
Jimmy Deoquino, Designer • **Jed Keith,** Social Media • **Jerrod Clark,** Publicity

ACT

PHILOS

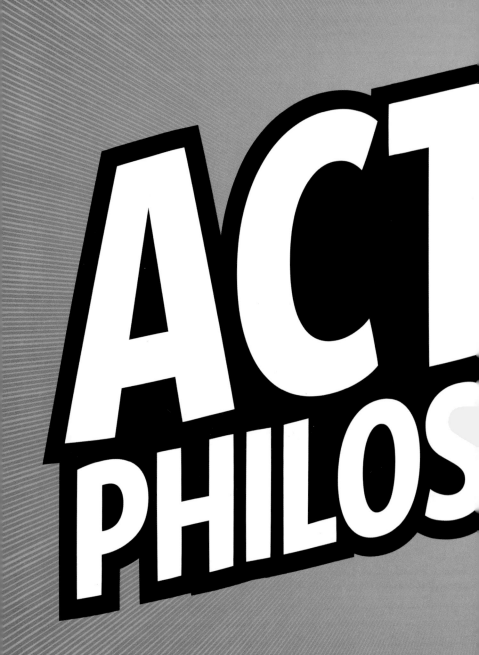

...ION
...OPHERS

HOOKED ON CLASSICS

FRED VAN LENTE - writer
RYAN DUNLAVEY - artist
ADAM GUZOWSKI - colorist

TABLE OF CONTENTS

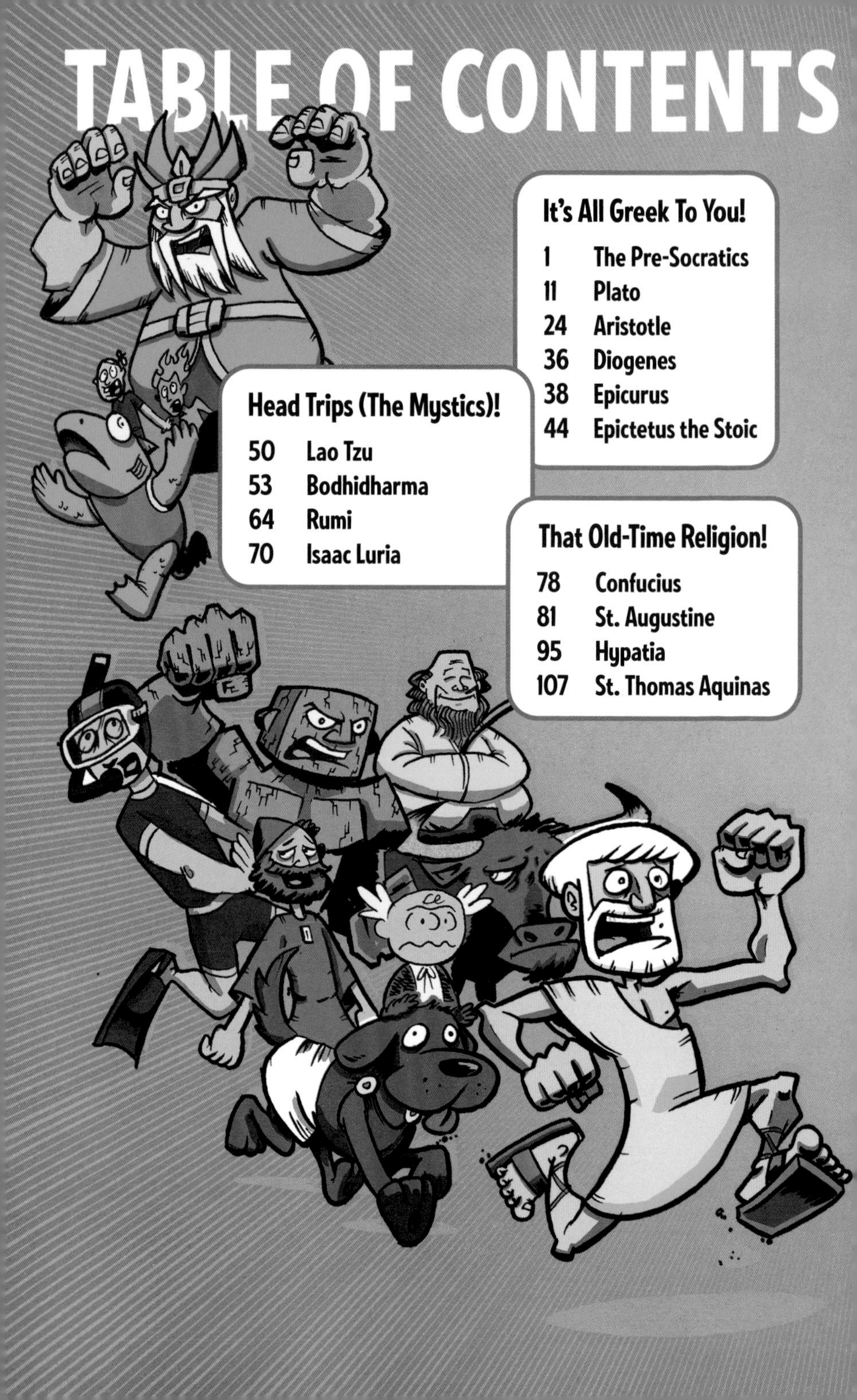

"Philosophy is not a ***theory***, but an ***activity***."

-Ludwig Wittgenstein

Tractatus Logico-Philosophicus

IT'S ALL GREECE TO YOU

THRACE

MACEDON

EPIRUS

LESBOS

DELPHI

ATHENS

TO MT. ETNA
(IN SICILY)

TO MILETUS &
EPHESUS
(ON COAST OF TURKEY)

SPARTA

TO CITIUM
(S.E. CYPRUS)

CRETE

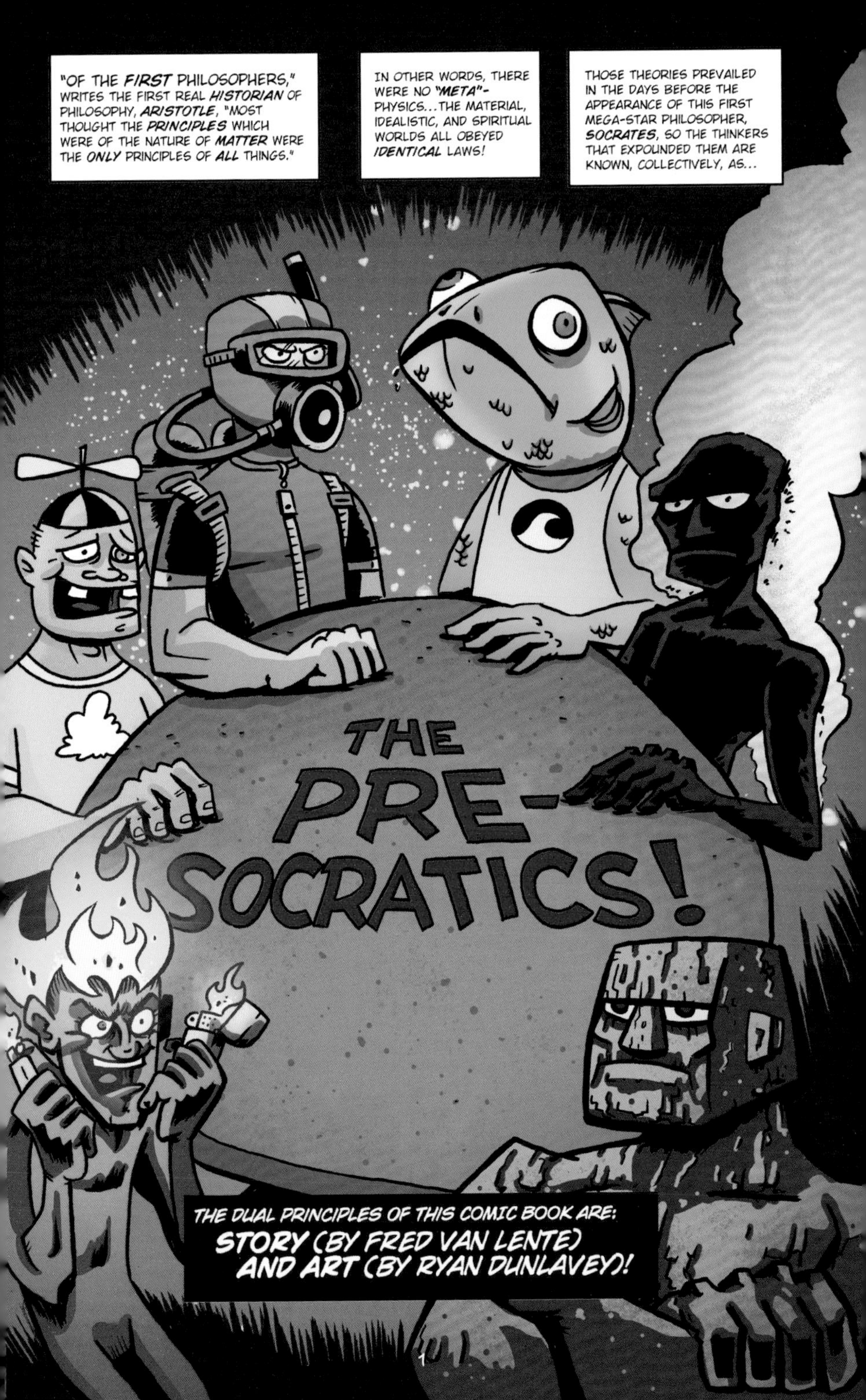
"OF THE FIRST PHILOSOPHERS," WRITES THE FIRST REAL HISTORIAN OF PHILOSOPHY, ARISTOTLE, "MOST THOUGHT THE PRINCIPLES WHICH WERE OF THE NATURE OF MATTER WERE THE ONLY PRINCIPLES OF ALL THINGS."
IN OTHER WORDS, THERE WERE NO "META"-PHYSICS... THE MATERIAL, IDEALISTIC, AND SPIRITUAL WORLDS ALL OBEYED IDENTICAL LAWS!
THOSE THEORIES PREVAILED IN THE DAYS BEFORE THE APPEARANCE OF THIS FIRST MEGA-STAR PHILOSOPHER, SOCRATES, SO THE THINKERS THAT EXPOUNDED THEM ARE KNOWN, COLLECTIVELY, AS...
THE PRE-SOCRATICS!
THE DUAL PRINCIPLES OF THIS COMIC BOOK ARE:
STORY (BY FRED VAN LENTE)
AND ART (BY RYAN DUNLAVEY)!

THALES OF MILETUS!

THALES WAS A SCIENTIFIC *JACK-OF-ALL-TRADES.* HE PREDICTED *ECLIPSES*, DIVERTED THE FLOW OF MIGHTY *RIVERS*...

...AND FIGURED OUT HOW TO MEASURE THE HEIGHT OF THE *PYRAMIDS* BY MEASURING THEIR *SHADOWS* AT THE PRECISE TIME OF DAY WHEN *HIS* SHADOW WAS EQUAL TO *HIS* HEIGHT!

YOU'D THINK HIS MAD *MENTAL SKILLS* WOULD HAVE WON THALES SOME *PROPS* FROM HIS PEEPS.

YOU'D BE *WRONG*...

PFFF! SHADOW BOY HERE THINKS HE'S SO *GREAT!*

IF YOU'RE SO *SMART*, WHY AREN'T YOU *RICH*, POINDEXTER? *HAW, HAW!*

AFTER CAREFUL *STUDY*, THALES DETERMINED THAT THE FOLLOWING SUMMER WOULD PRODUCE AN ESPECIALLY BOUNTIFUL *OLIVE* CROP, SO HE USED HIS LAST CENT TO BUY UP ALL THE OLIVE *PRESSES* IN THE NEIGHBORHOOD!

ONCE HIS PREDICTION CAME *TRUE*, HE *CLEANED UP* RENTING OUT HIS EQUIPMENT TO THE GROWERS!

WHO *SAYS* PHILOSOPHY DOESN'T *PAY?* HEH!

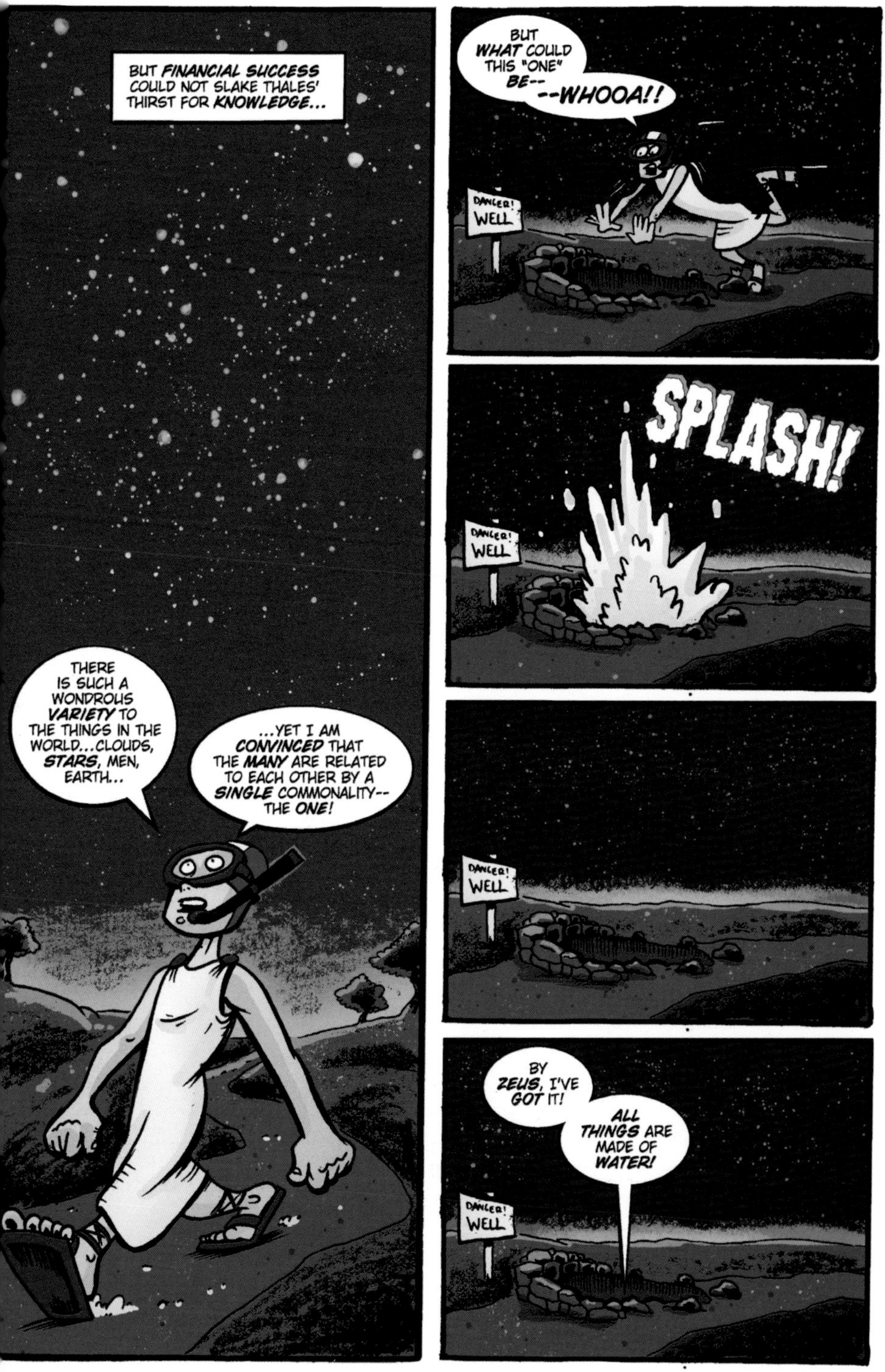
BUT FINANCIAL SUCCESS COULD NOT SLAKE THALES' THIRST FOR KNOWLEDGE...
THERE IS SUCH A WONDROUS VARIETY TO THE THINGS IN THE WORLD...CLOUDS, STARS, MEN, EARTH...
...YET I AM CONVINCED THAT THE MANY ARE RELATED TO EACH OTHER BY A SINGLE COMMONALITY-- THE ONE!
BUT WHAT COULD THIS "ONE" BE--
--WHOOA!!
DANGER! WELL
SPLASH!
DANGER! WELL
DANGER! WELL
BY ZEUS, I'VE GOT IT!
ALL THINGS ARE MADE OF WATER!
DANGER! WELL

ANAXIMANDER!

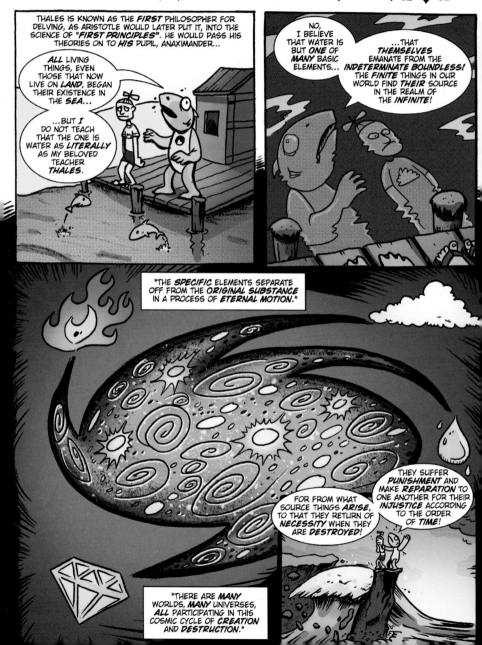

THALES IS KNOWN AS THE *FIRST* PHILOSOPHER FOR DELVING, AS ARISTOTLE WOULD LATER PUT IT, INTO THE SCIENCE OF *"FIRST PRINCIPLES"*. HE WOULD PASS HIS THEORIES ON TO *HIS* PUPIL, ANAXIMANDER...

ALL LIVING THINGS, EVEN THOSE THAT NOW LIVE ON *LAND*, BEGAN THEIR EXISTENCE IN THE *SEA*...

...BUT *I* DO NOT TEACH THAT THE ONE IS WATER AS *LITERALLY* AS MY BELOVED TEACHER *THALES*.

NO, I BELIEVE THAT WATER IS BUT *ONE* OF *MANY* BASIC ELEMENTS...

...THAT *THEMSELVES* EMANATE FROM THE *INDETERMINATE BOUNDLESS!* THE *FINITE* THINGS IN OUR WORLD FIND *THEIR* SOURCE IN THE REALM OF THE *INFINITE!*

"THE *SPECIFIC* ELEMENTS SEPARATE OFF FROM THE *ORIGINAL SUBSTANCE* IN A PROCESS OF *ETERNAL MOTION.*"

THEY SUFFER *PUNISHMENT* AND MAKE *REPARATION* TO ONE ANOTHER FOR THEIR *INJUSTICE* ACCORDING TO THE ORDER OF *TIME!*

FOR FROM WHAT SOURCE THINGS *ARISE*, TO THAT THEY RETURN OF *NECESSITY* WHEN THEY ARE *DESTROYED!*

"THERE ARE *MANY* WORLDS, *MANY* UNIVERSES, *ALL* PARTICIPATING IN THIS COSMIC CYCLE OF *CREATION* AND *DESTRUCTION.*"

ANAXIMENES!

NOW... *I* RETURN TO THE INDETERMINATE BOUNDLESS... COUGH!

I TRUST *YOU* WILL CARRY ON MY TEACHINGS, ANAXIMENES... ÷GAK!÷

YEAH, *RIGHT!* IN YOUR *DREAMS*, POPS!

YOUR *THEORIES* STINK ALMOST AS BAD AS YOUR *FEET!*

ANYBODY WITH HALF A *BRAIN* COULD SEE THE FIRST CAUSE ISN'T *WATER*--

Kick!

OR YOUR WACKY *INDETERMINATE BOUNDLESS...*

...BUT *AIR!* WHILE IT IS *INVISIBLE*, LIKE OUR VERY *SOULS*, ITS MOVEMENTS MAY BE TRACKED SCIENTIFICALLY!

ALL THE OTHER ELEMENTS *DERIVE* FROM AIR! WHEN SPED *UP*, AIR FORMS *FIRE*, AND WHEN SLOWED *DOWN*, IT FORMS *WATER!*

SO WAS INAUGURATED ONE OF THE MOST *COMMON* PHILOSOPHICAL TRADITIONS:

EVERY PHILOSOPHER WHO CAME BEFORE *ME* WAS AN *IDIOT!*

HERACLITUS!

HEIR TO THE THRONE OF *EPHESUS*, HERACLITUS CEDED HIS CROWN TO HIS *BROTHER* SO HE'D HAVE MORE TIME FOR *THOUGHT*.

UH... SOME MIGHT SAY YOU'RE NOT THINKIN' TOO STRAIGHT RIGHT *NOW*, BRO'...

"ALL THINGS ARE IN FLUX" WAS HIS CATCHPHRASE, MORE *FAMOUSLY* FORMULATED AS:

"YOU CANNOT STEP TWICE INTO THE SAME RIVER."

FOR THE SECOND TIME IT'S NOT THE SAME *RIVER*, AND YOU'RE NOT THE SAME *MAN*.

FIRE, ACCORDING TO HERACLITUS, IS THAT CONSTANT ELEMENT IN *ALL* THINGS THAT *CHANGES*--THE *"UNITY* IN *DIVERSITY!"*

OOOHHH... PRETTY...

BUT THIS IS NOT MERELY ANOTHER VERSION OF "THE ONE" AS TAUGHT BY THALES OR ANAXIMENES, BUT A PROCESS OF *TRANSFORMATION!*

THE WORLD IS, HERACLITUS SAYS, AN *"EVER-LIVING FIRE"* WHICH IS MAINTAINED BY *"MEASURES OF IT KINDLING AND MEASURES GOING OUT."*

"ALL THINGS ARE AN EXCHANGE FOR FIRE, AND FIRE FOR ALL THINGS, EVEN AS WARES FOR GOLD AND GOLD FOR WARES."

NOTHING IS EVER *DESTROYED,* BUT MERELY CONVERTS TO A DIFFERENT *FORM!* THIS NOTION IS REMARKABLY SIMILAR TO PHYSICS' NOTION OF THE CONSERVATION OF MATTER AND ENERGY.

OOOHHH... PRETTY...

HENCE WE HAVE *STABILITY* IN THE UNIVERSE NOT IN *SPITE* OF, BUT *BECAUSE* OF CONSTANT *CHANGE!*

GOD *IS* FIRE, AND GOD-FIRE PERMEATES *ALL* THINGS--INCLUDING THE HUMAN *SOUL!*

REASON IS THE *FIRE* OF THE SOUL, FOR ONLY THROUGH *IT* CAN WE SEE THAT WHICH IS SHARED BY ALL *THINGS!*

THUS, THOUGH MEN ARE ALL *DIFFERENT,* THEY ARE *UNITED* BY A *SINGLE* FLAME!

AND THOUGH MEN ALWAYS *DISAGREE,* *"WHAT IS IN OPPOSITION IS IN CONCERT AND FROM WHAT DIFFERS COMES THE MOST BEAUTIFUL HARMONY."*

JUST AS *FIRE* IS THE CONSTANT IN *CHANGE,* IT IS ONLY THROUGH THE TENSION BETWEEN *OPPOSITES* THAT THE UNIVERSE ACHIEVES *ORDER!*

IF THAT SOUNDS LIKE *TOTAL B.S.* TO YOU, YOU'RE NOT *ALONE!*

I'VE ALWAYS FOUND THE WHOLE *NOTION* OF CHANGE TO BE COMPLETELY *ILLOGICAL!*

I MEAN-- *REALLY!* THALES AND HERACLITUS BOTH GO *ON AND ON* ABOUT THIS PROCESS OF *"BECOMING"*...

...BUT I *ASK* YOU, HAVE YOU EVER *SEEN* SOMETHING IN THE PROCESS OF *BECOMING?*

OF *COURSE* NOT! A THING EITHER *IS* OR IT *ISN'T!*

THAT'S THE FUNDAMENTAL *UNDERLYING* CONCEPT OF TH PHILOSOPHY OF...

"BECOMING" ⟷ "IS"

PARMENIDES!

"ONE PATH *ONLY* IS LEFT FOR US TO SPEAK OF, NAMELY, THAT *IT IS.* IN THIS PATH ARE VERY MANY TOKENS THAT WHAT IS, IS UNCREATED AND *INDESTRUCTIBLE,* FOR IT IS COMPLETE, UNMOVABLE AND *WITHOUT END.*"

THERE IS *NO* CHANGE OR MOTION -- THESE ARE MERELY *ILLUSIONS* PRODUCED BY OUR *SENSES!*

THOUGH THINGS MAY ALTER IN *APPEARANCE,* THEY REMAIN, IN ESSENCE, EXACTLY THE *SAME!*

PARMENIDES' STUDENT *ZENO* ILLUSTRATED THE ILLUSION OF *MOTION* WITH HIS FAMOUS *PARADOX:*

½ of ½ WAY

½ WAY MARK

IF YOU'RE RUNNING A RACE, YOU CAN'T REACH THE *FINISH* WITHOUT GETTING *HALFWAY* THERE, RIGHT-- AND YOU CAN'T *THERE* WITHOUT GETTING HALFWAY TO *HALFWAY,* RIGHT--AND YOU CAN'T GET TO HALFWAY TO HALFWAY WITHOUT GETTING *HALF WAY*-- SO...THE QUESTION *IS...*

...HOW DOES *ANYONE* GET *ANYWHERE?*

SEE?

THE ONE CAN NEVER BE *DIVIDED* INTO ITS SEPARATE *PARTS,* SUCH AS *ELEMENTS* OR *PRIMARY* AND LESSER *CAUSES!*

LIKEWISE, NOTHING EVER *CHANGES!* NOT EVEN THIS *COMIC BOOK STORY!* IT WILL JUST GO *ON* AND *ON* AND *ON* AND--

8

EMPEDOCLES!

LEGEND HAS IT EMPEDOCLES WANTED TO BE REMEMBERED AS A *GOD*, SO HE LEAPT INTO THE VOLCANO AT *MT. ETNA* TO ERASE ALL TRACE OF HIS *BODY*.

WHY CAN'T PHILOSOPHERS JUST GET *ALONG*?

I FIGURED OUT A WAY *NONE* OF US CAN BE WRONG!

PARMENIDES WAS CORRECT WHEN HE SAID WHAT *IS* ALWAYS *WAS*;

BUT HERACLITUS WAS RIGHT *TOO* THAT WITH *CHANGE* THE UNIVERSE IS ALWAYS *ABUZZ*!

I SAY IT'S THE *ELEMENTS* THAT MAKE *UP* THE *ONE* THAT ARE ALWAYS IN *FLUX*.

THALES SAID IT WAS *WATER*, ANAXIMENES SAID IT WAS *AIR*.... I SAY THEY'RE *BOTH* RIGHT, THE BRAINY YOUNG BUCKS!

WIND AND WATER ARE BUT *TWO* OF THE *FOUR* THAT MAKE UP ALL THE WORLD'S *MATTER. FIRE* AND *EARTH* ROUND OUT THAT QUARTET--

--AND THUS ENDS MY PHILOSOPHICAL PATTER!

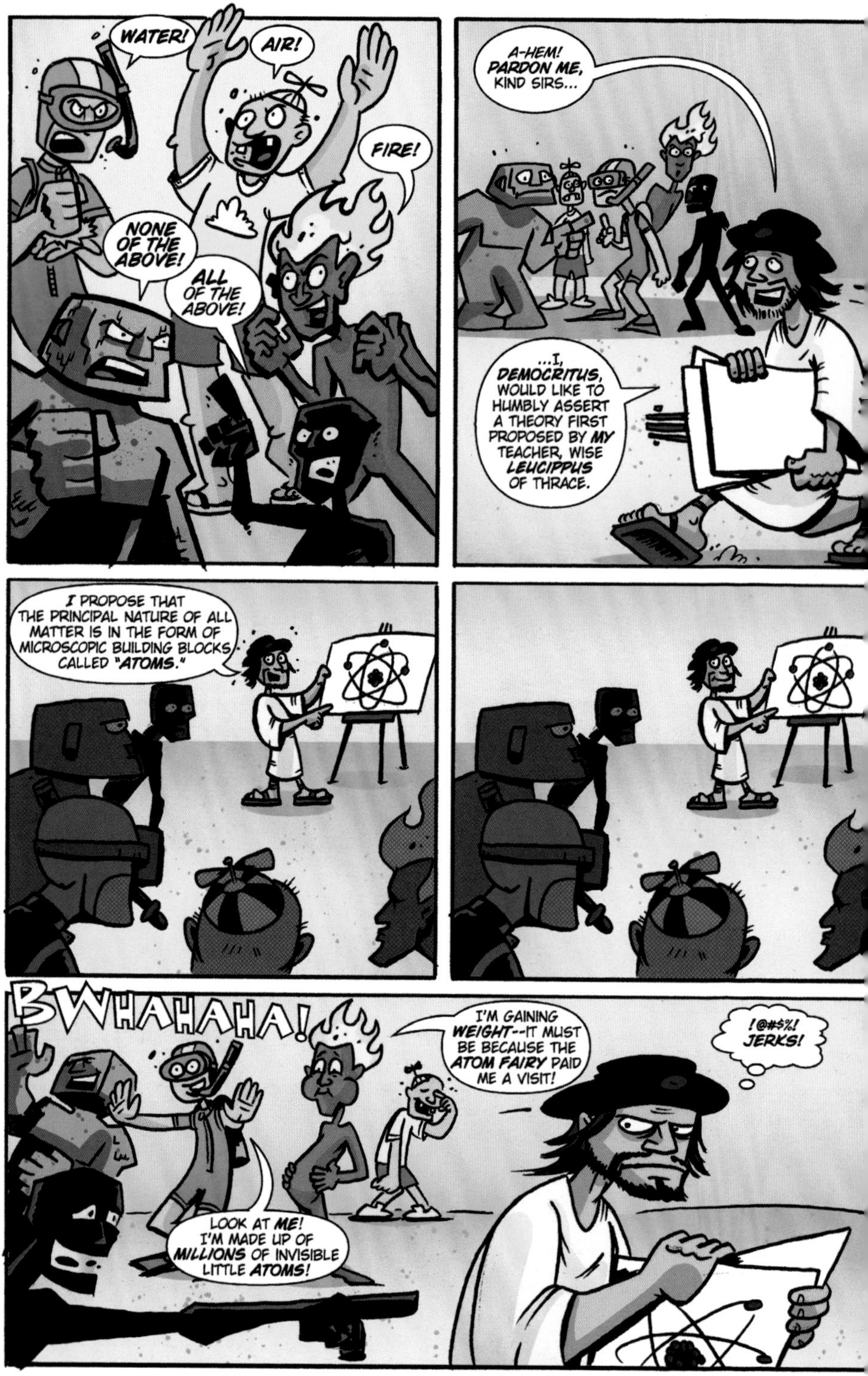

WATER!
AIR!
FIRE!
NONE OF THE ABOVE!
ALL OF THE ABOVE!
A-HEM! PARDON ME, KIND SIRS...
...I, DEMOCRITUS, WOULD LIKE TO HUMBLY ASSERT A THEORY FIRST PROPOSED BY MY TEACHER, WISE LEUCIPPUS OF THRACE.
I PROPOSE THAT THE PRINCIPAL NATURE OF ALL MATTER IS IN THE FORM OF MICROSCOPIC BUILDING BLOCKS CALLED "ATOMS."
BWHAHAHA!
LOOK AT ME! I'M MADE UP OF MILLIONS OF INVISIBLE LITTLE ATOMS!
I'M GAINING WEIGHT--IT MUST BE BECAUSE THE ATOM FAIRY PAID ME A VISIT!
!@#$%! JERKS!

MEET ACTION PHILOSOPHER #1: PLATO!

"PLATO" MEANS "BROAD" OR "FLAT" AND WAS THE *STAGE NAME* OF A PRO WRESTLER BORN *ARISTOCLES* ON THE ISLAND OF AEGINA IN 428 B.C.!

APPARENTLY HE ADOPTED THIS *NOM DE GUERRE* BECAUSE OF HIS EXCEPTIONALLY BROAD *SHOULDERS.**

(*: YES, *REALLY.*)

THOUGH TWO-TIME CHAMP OF THE *ISTHMIAN GAMES*, PLATO NEVER QUALIFIED FOR THE *OLYMPICS*, NECESSITATING A CAREER SWITCH.

PLATO'S MIGHTY HEART *BREAKING...*

YOU SUCK

CLOSED

WHILE DABBLING IN POETRY AND POLITICS IN *ATHENS*, MR. BROAD FELL IN WITH THE WANDERING SAGE *SOCRATES* AND HIS YOUTHFUL STUDENTS.

SOCRATES GOT INTO THE PHILOSOPHY RACKET WHEN FAMED *"PSYCHIC FRIEND"* THE *ORACLE AT DELPHI* TOLD HIM...

NO MAN IS AS WISE AS SOCRATES!

COOL!

CALL NOW!

ONLY $3.99/MINUTE

1-900-4ORACLE

HE WENT ABOUT *PROVING* THIS BY SHOOTING DOWN ATHENIAN CONVENTIONAL WISDOM IN BACK-AND-FORTH *"DIALECTIC"* CRITIQUES:

SO IF RELIGION IS B.S., THEN *YOU* TELL ME: WHAT *IS* TRUTH?

I DO NOT *KNOW.*

WHAT? THEN HOW CAN YOU BE *WISER* THAN EVERYBODY ELSE?

BECAUSE I *KNOW* THAT I DO NOT KNOW.

BY ZEUS, YOU'RE A *PAIN IN THE ASS.*

SOCRATES ENCOURAGED HIS *STUDENTS* TO GET IN THE ACT, AND YOU KNOW HOW MUCH YOUNG PEOPLE *HATE* SHOWING UP THEIR ELDERS...

IF YOU BOYS ARE SEARCHING FOR *TRUTH,* YOU SHOULD LOOK TO *ZEUS!*

ARE ZEUS'S ACTIONS *ARBITRARY,* OR IS *HE* GUIDED BY TRUTH TOO?

OF COURSE ZEUS IS GUIDED BY TRUTH!

WELL, IN *THAT* CASE, *I* SHOULD JUST LOOK FOR *TRUTH...*

...FOR A *WISE* MAN WOULD NOT *NEED* ZEUS!

≥GASP! CHOKE!≥

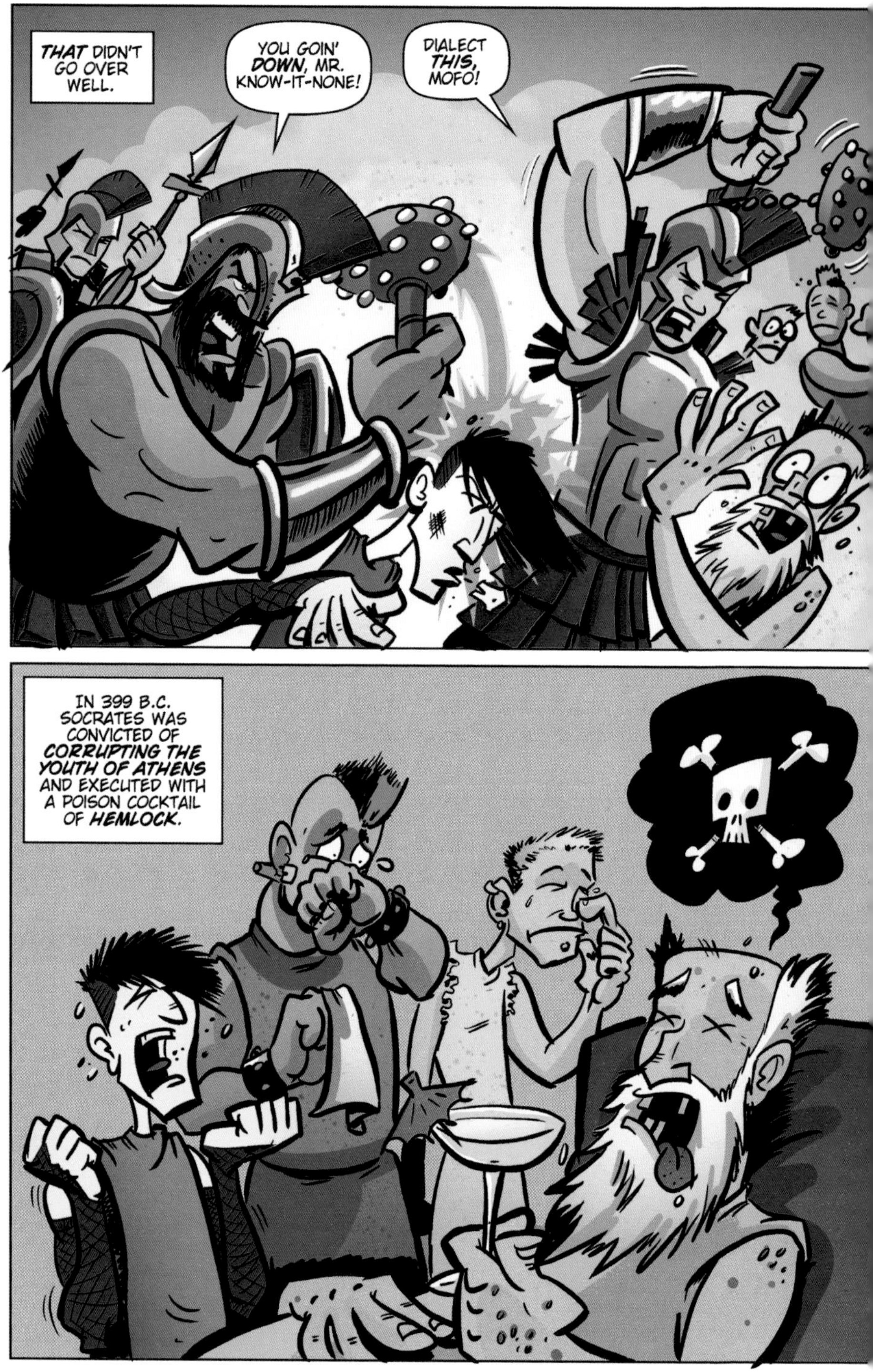
THAT DIDN'T GO OVER WELL.
YOU GOIN' DOWN, MR. KNOW-IT-NONE!
DIALECT THIS, MOFO!
IN 399 B.C. SOCRATES WAS CONVICTED OF CORRUPTING THE YOUTH OF ATHENS AND EXECUTED WITH A POISON COCKTAIL OF HEMLOCK.

PLATO WOULD CALL SOCRATES' DEATH THE **TURNING POINT** OF HIS LIFE.

BUT ATHENS WAS NO LONGER A **SAFE PLACE** FOR SOCRATIC STUDENTS! HE WANDERED THE MEDITERRANEAN WORLD IN EXILE FOR OVER A DECADE...

...FINALLY ENDING UP IN **SICILY**, WHERE HE ENCOUNTERED A SECT OF **PYTHAGOREANS**.

PYTHAGORAS--HE OF **TRIANGLE THEOREM** FAME—FOUNDED A BIZARRE CULT OF **MATH HIPPIES** IN THE 6TH CENTURY B.C. WHO BELIEVED THEY COULD COMPREHEND THE NATURE OF THE COSMOS THROUGH **NUMBERS**.

TO PURIFY THEIR MINDS FOR MYSTIC **CALCULATIONS**, THE PYTHAGOREANS TOOK A VOW OF **SECRECY**, COULD ONLY WEAR **WHITE**...

...AND SWORE OFF **SEXUAL INTERCOURSE**.

THAT LAST ONE –>**HEH!**<– SHOULDN'T BE MUCH OF A **CHALLENGE!**

SOME OF THE CULT'S *OTHER* TENETS WERE RATHER, ER, *UNIQUE*...

...LIKE A PROHIBITION AGAINST TOUCHING *BEANS*.

"ALL IS NUMBER" WAS THEIR WATCHWORD...

...MEANING OUR MESSY, MATERIAL UNIVERSE IS THE IMPERFECT *EXPRESSION* OF A HIGHER, ABSTRACT UNIVERSE...

...A PERFECT AND HARMONIOUS REALM OF *NUMBER*.

OHHHHH... REALM OF *NUMBERS*...

WAIT! PLATO KNOWS *HE* KNOW WHAT SOCRATES KNEW HE DID *NOT* KNOW!

POOF!

WELL WHADAYA KNOW?

EXPOSURE TO THIS THEORY LED PLATO TO THE CONCLUSION THAT REAL TRUTH WAS *ABSTRACT*, AND, LIKE NUMBERS, UNCHANGING-- *ETERNAL!*

ALL *CHAIRS*, FOR EXAMPLE, ARE SIMPLY THE EXPRESSION OF THE *IDEA* OF A CHAIR—AND THOUGH OUR *"REAL"* CHAIRS ARE FLAWED AND *TEMPORARY*...

16

...THE IDEA OR *FORM* OF A CHAIR IS ETERNAL AND *UNCHANGING!*

OHHHHH... REALM OF *FORMS*...

PLATO ILLUSTRATED THE RELATIONSHIP OF FORMS TO *OUR* WORLD THUSLY:

"IMAGINE THE CONDITION OF MEN AS LIVING IN A SORT OF UNDERGROUND CAVERN."

"HERE MEN CAN ONLY SEE IN FRONT OF THEM."

"HIGHER UP, AND SOME DISTANCE BEHIND THEM, IS THE LIGHT OF A BURNING FIRE."

"BETWEEN THE FIRE AND THE MEN IS A PARAPET. BEHIND THE PARAPET IMAGINE THERE ARE MEN CARRYING ALL KINDS OF OBJECTS—INCLUDING FIGURES OF MEN AND ANIMALS—WHICH PROJECT ABOVE THE PARAPET."

"IN ALL WAYS, MEN WOULD CONSIDER REALITY TO BE NOTHING ELSE THAN THE SHADOWS OF THOSE ARTIFICIAL OBJECTS!"

Cine PLEX

ORM OF ALITY! REALITY!

I.M.N. FORM OF

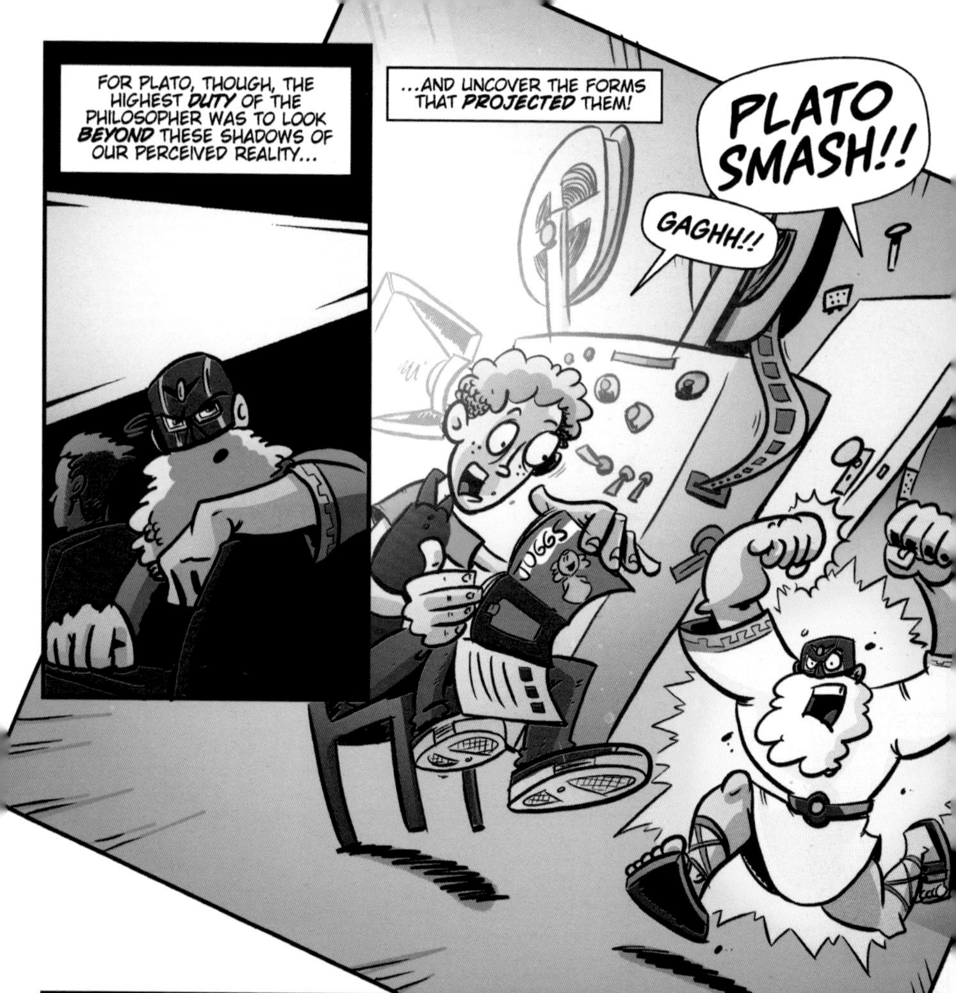
FOR PLATO, THOUGH, THE HIGHEST DUTY OF THE PHILOSOPHER WAS TO LOOK BEYOND THESE SHADOWS OF OUR PERCEIVED REALITY...
...AND UNCOVER THE FORMS THAT PROJECTED THEM!
PLATO SMASH!!
GAGHH!!
JUGGS

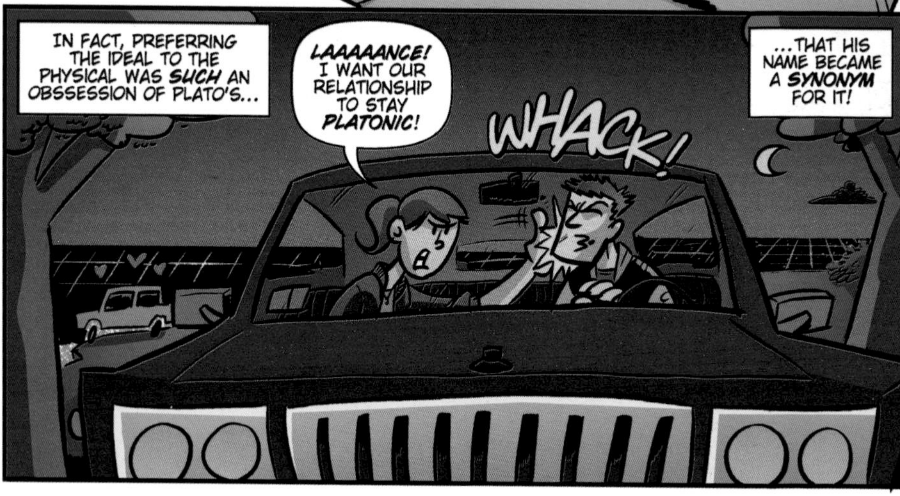
IN FACT, PREFERRING THE IDEAL TO THE PHYSICAL WAS SUCH AN OBSSESSION OF PLATO'S...
LAAAAAANCE! I WANT OUR RELATIONSHIP TO STAY PLATONIC!
WHACK!
...THAT HIS NAME BECAME A SYNONYM FOR IT!

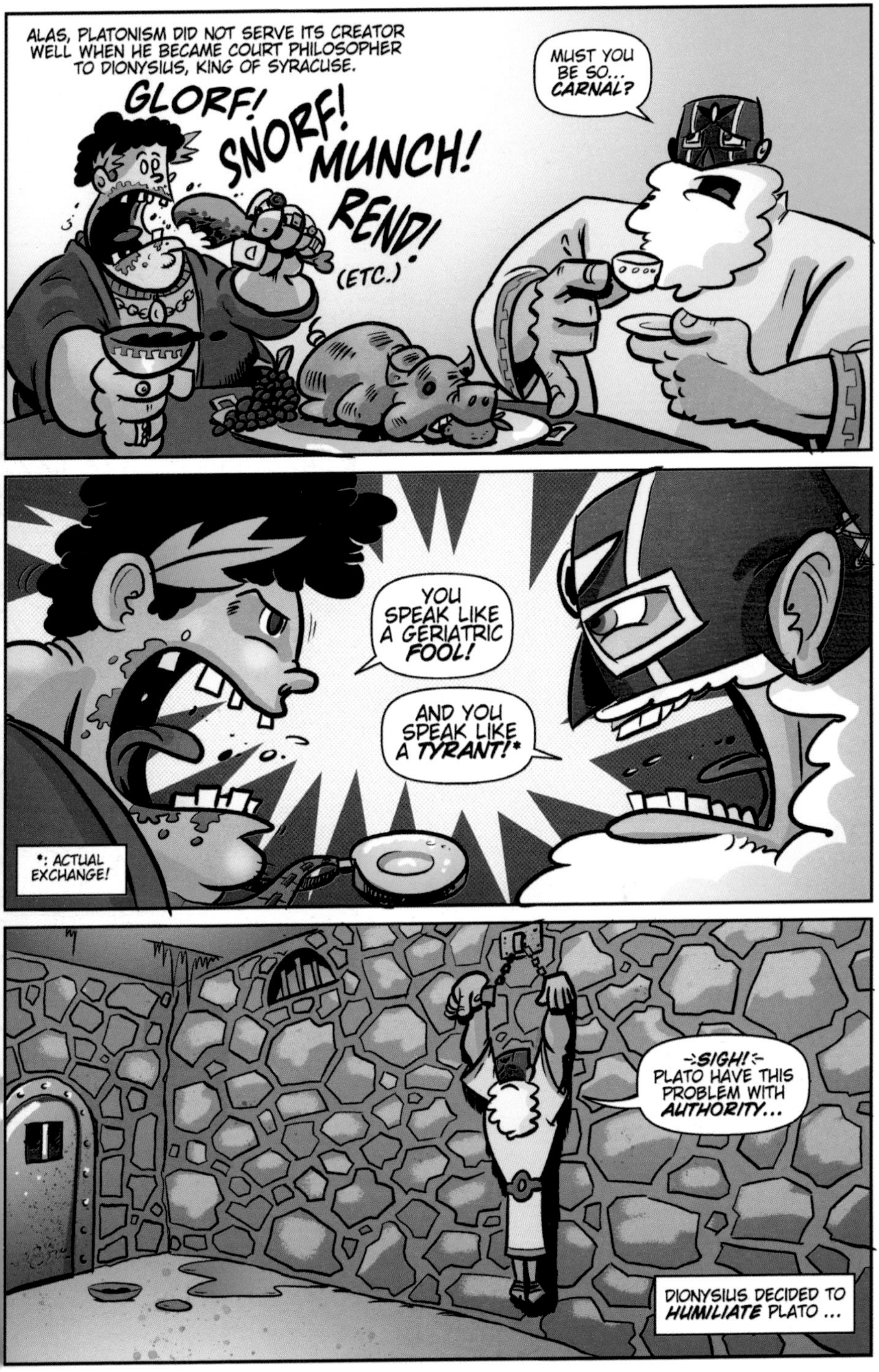
ALAS, PLATONISM DID NOT SERVE ITS CREATOR WELL WHEN HE BECAME COURT PHILOSOPHER TO DIONYSIUS, KING OF SYRACUSE.
GLORF! SNORF! MUNCH! REND! (ETC.)
MUST YOU BE SO... CARNAL?
YOU SPEAK LIKE A GERIATRIC FOOL!
AND YOU SPEAK LIKE A TYRANT!*
*: ACTUAL EXCHANGE!
SIGH! PLATO HAVE THIS PROBLEM WITH AUTHORITY...
DIONYSIUS DECIDED TO HUMILIATE PLATO ...

...BY SELLING HIM INTO **SLAVERY** TO HIS HOMETOWN OF AEGINA ...

PLATO DO **ANYTHING,** JUST DON'T WANT TO GET **REAL JOB!!**

LOT #42 1 Philosopher. USED.

...WHERE, FORTUITOUSLY, A **BUDDY** BOUGHT HIS FREEDOM.

HIS BENEFACTOR ALSO GAVE HIM ENOUGH DOUGH TO SET UP A **SCHOOL** JUST OUTSIDE ATHENS.

PLATO NAME IT AFTER FORMER RESIDENT OF NEIGHBORHOOD, **HERO HECADEMUS!**

AND SO **THE ACADEMY** OPENED ITS DOORS IN 387 B.C.!

AT THE ACADEMY, PLATO DIVESTED PYTHAGORISM OF ITS MONDO-BIZARRO RITUALS...

...AND GAVE THE SOCRATICS' KNEEJERK CRITIQUING THE THEORY OF FORMS AS AN OPERATING **VALUE SYSTEM,** THEREBY CREATING ...

...COLLEGE!

LIKE ANY GOOD PROFESSOR, PLATO **PUBLISHED** WIDELY AS WELL.

AGAIN?!

OFFICE HOURS CANCELLED

BUT I GOTTA TALK ABOUT MY INDEPENDENT STUDY!

PLATO'S WORKS TAKE THE FORM OF **DIALOGUES,** OR DISCUSSIONS BETWEEN TEACHER AND STUDENT. INVARIABLY THE TEACHER IS **SOCRATES** HIMSELF, RESURRECTED BY PLATO TO MOUTH HIS OWN THEORIES—AND GIVE THEM ADDED **LEGITIMACY!**

SOCRATES

BRAINS!! MUST...USE... BRAINS!!

IN *THE APOLOGY* PLATO TRANSFORMS TRANSIENT CRACKPOT SOCRATES INTO HISTORY'S FIRST *LIBERAL MARTYR!*

SINCE I DO NOT *KNOW* WHAT COMES AFTER DEATH, WHY SHOULD I *FEAR* IT? --CHUCKLE!--

HIS WITTY HUMANISM TRUMPS OUR STAID ADHEARANCE TO TRADITION! --CHOKE!--

HE'S *RIGHT*--BUT BECAUSE HE'S AN AFFRONT TO OUR POWER--WE HAVE TO KILL HIM *ANYWAY!*

PLATO'S ACADEMY THRIVED FOR *CENTURIES* AS A CENTER FOR MATHEMATICS AND ETHICS—TWO SUBJECTS DEPENDANT ON *ABSOLUTES!*

BUT IN HIS DIALOGUE *THE REPUBLIC*, PLATO HIMSELF TRIED USING THE *SAME* ABSOLUTES TO PROPOSE THE PERFECT *SOCIETY.*

HERE CHILDREN WOULD BE TAKEN FROM THEIR MOTHERS AT *BIRTH* AND RAISED IN STATE ORPHANAGES, SO THEY WOULD THINK OF THE *GOVERNMENT* AS THEIR PARENTS.

MA-MA! DA-DA!

SCHOOLING DETERMINED A CITIZEN'S PLACE IN SOCIETY. ALL THOSE WHO FLUNKED *GYM* BECAME *FARMERS* TO GROW FOOD FOR THE GOOD OF ALL.

--PANT!--
--PANT!--

!@#$%! *DODGEBALL!*

IF YOU PASSED GYM BUT FLUNKED *MATH*, YOU'D ENTER THE *MILITARY.*

THERE'S 3,000 OF *THEM*--AND ONE--PLUS ONE PLUS ONE OF *US!*

WE OUTNUMBER THEM!!

GET 'EM, BOYS!!!

BUT IF YOU EXCELLED AT GYM *AND* MATH, YOU WERE ONE OF THE *ELITE*, DESTINED TO *LEAD* THE REPUBLIC, AND YOU WOULD GET TO STUDY--

--*WAIT* FOR IT--

--PHILOSOPHY! (SURPRISED?)

THESE PHILOSOPHER-RULERS WOULD *SLEEP* TOGETHER, *WORK* TOGETHER, AND SHARE *ALL* POSSESSIONS...

...AND THIS WOULD KEEP THEM FREE OF *CORRUPTION.*

(POLITICAL CORRUPTION, THAT IS.)

ONE WOULD BE CHOSEN TO BE THE *PHILOSOPHER-KING* WHO WOULD RULE OVER ALL.

ALL MUSIC AND LITERATURE THAT DID NOT PRAISE THE STATE WOULD BE BANNED--ALL INDIVIDUALISM WOULD BE UTTERLY *ERADICATED.*

PLATO WOULD HAVE FORCED HUMAN *SOCIETY* TO ADHERE TO THE *IMPOSSIBLE,* ABSTRACT STANDARD OF THE REALM OF FORMS!

IN 367 B.C. PLATO WAS OFFERED AN OPPORTUNITY TO *REALIZE* HIS DEMENTED BRAND OF HOMOEROTIC FASCISM...

DUDE! COME BACK TO SYRACUSE! DIONYSUS IS *DEAD!*

HMM...

WE CAN SET THE REPUBLIC UP *THERE,* IT'LL BE AWESOME!

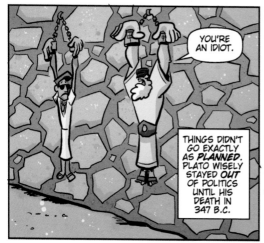

YOU'RE AN IDIOT.

THINGS DIDN'T GO EXACTLY AS *PLANNED.* PLATO WISELY STAYED *OUT* OF POLITICS UNTIL HIS DEATH IN 347 B.C.

THE CHRISTIAN EMPEROR JUSTINIAN SHUT DOWN THE ACADEMY IN A.D. 529, BECAUSE IT WAS TOO *ATHEISTIC* FOR HIM.

THIS EVENT IS USUALLY USED TO DEMARCATE THE START OF *THE DARK AGES.*

OUT OF BUSINESS

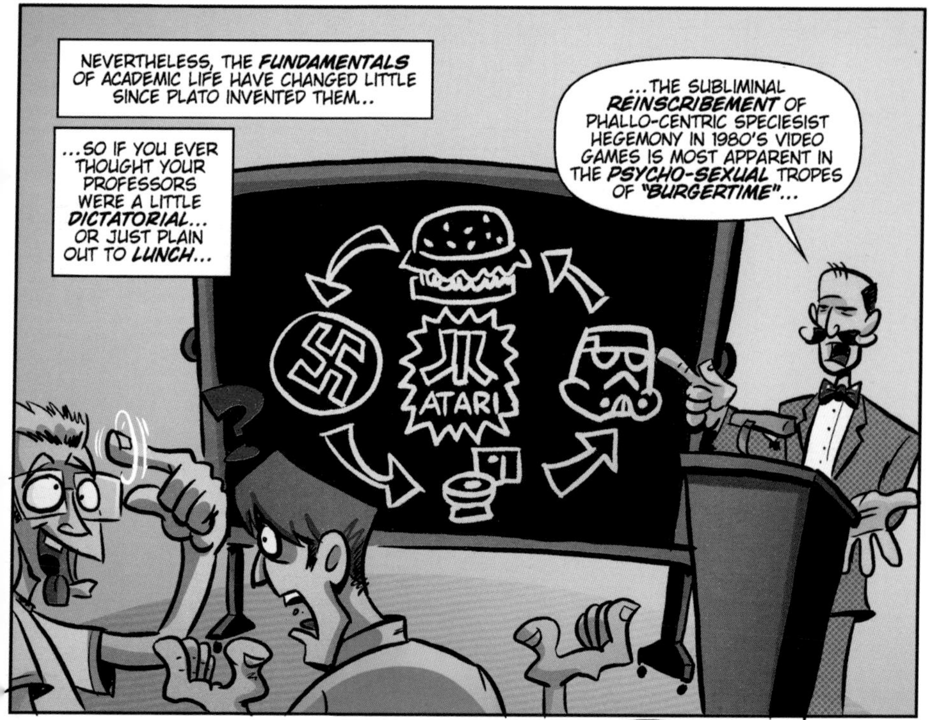
NEVERTHELESS, THE FUNDAMENTALS OF ACADEMIC LIFE HAVE CHANGED LITTLE SINCE PLATO INVENTED THEM...
...SO IF YOU EVER THOUGHT YOUR PROFESSORS WERE A LITTLE DICTATORIAL... OR JUST PLAIN OUT TO LUNCH...
...THE SUBLIMINAL REINSCRIBEMENT OF PHALLO-CENTRIC SPECIESIST HEGEMONY IN 1980'S VIDEO GAMES IS MOST APPARENT IN THE PSYCHO-SEXUAL TROPES OF "BURGERTIME"...
ATARI

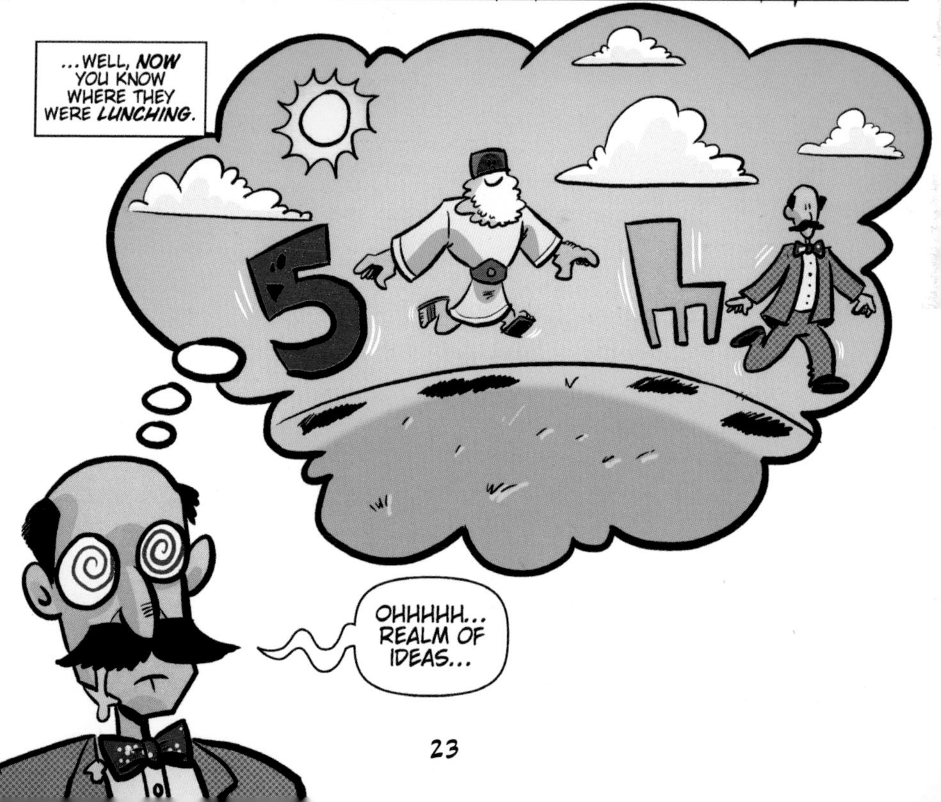
...WELL, NOW YOU KNOW WHERE THEY WERE LUNCHING.
OHHHHH... REALM OF IDEAS...

PLATO, FOUNDER OF THE ATHENIAN ACADEMY, DIED IN *347 B.C.*, AND MANY FEARED THAT HIS TRADITION OF THINKING AND LEARNING MIGHT DIE *WITH* HIM.

NO ONE YET REALIZED THAT *ACTION PHILOSOPHER #20* WAITED IN THE WINGS TO PICK UP THE TORCH...

ARISTOTLE!

LISTEN UP, PEOPLE! THOUGH WE'RE ALL STILL MOURNING MY *UNCLE*, I'D LIKE TO ANNOUNCE SOME CHANGES TO NEXT TERM'S *COURSE OFFERINGS*:

WE'RE REPLACING HISTORY WITH *PROBABILITY*-- LITERATURE WITH *GEOMETRY*-- AND, INSTEAD OF *RECESS*... ...CALCULUS!

NEW CURRICULUM: 'MATH 'MATH 'MORE MATH

SEE HERE, *SPEUSIPPUS!* I KNOW PLATO NAMED YOU HIS *SUCCESSOR...*

...BUT I'VE TAUGHT *BIOLOGY* AT THIS SCHOOL FOR ALMOST *TWENTY YEARS!* I DON'T SEE IT OFFERED *ANYWHERE* IN YOUR NEW COURSE CATALOG!

I *KNOW* WHO YOU ARE, ARISTOTLE...

...I *ALSO* KNOW YOU NEVER APPRECIATED THE *MATHEMATICAL BEAUTY* OF MY UNCLE'S THEORY OF *FORMS!*

WELL...*YES,* I PROTESTED HIS IDEA THAT THE FORMS ACTUALLY *EXIST* IN NATURE, THOUGH THERE IS NO *EMPIRICAL EVIDENCE* TO SUSTAIN SUCH A CLAIM--

~TSK!~ A *PITY.*

SAY, THAT *REMINDS* ME--WE'VE *REPLACED* BIOLOGY WITH *ACCOUNTING!*

IF YOU DON'T *LIKE* IT, I BELIEVE THERE'S A *HALL MONITOR* POSITION OPEN...

SON OF THE ROYAL PHYSICIAN TO THE COURT OF NEARBY *MACEDON,* ARISTOTLE HAD ARRIVED AT THE ACADEMY AS A 17-YEAR-OLD STUDENT AND NEVER *LEFT...*

SEE IF YOU CAN'T ADD *THIS* UP, SPEUSIPPUS...

...I QUIT!

...UNTIL *NOW!*

UNLIKE PLATO, HE BELIEVED THAT BEING WASN'T *STATIC,* BUT RATHER IN A CONSTANT STATE OF *CHANGE*--SO ONE COULD DRAW CONCLUSIONS ABOUT IT ONLY BY *OBSERVING* BEINGS IN ACTION IN NATURE.

AFTER LEAVING THE *ACADEMY,* HE EMBARKED ON A SERIES OF TEACHING GIGS AND SCIENTIFIC EXPEDITIONS TO VARIOUS PLACES AROUND THE HELLENIC WORLD, INCLUDING THE ISLAND OF *LESBOS.*

WHAT'S *HER* PROBLEM?

THEN, IN 343 B.C., HE RECEIVED A *ROYAL SUMMONS* FROM MACEDON'S *KING PHILIP II:*

YOU SHALL COME *TUTOR* THE *HEIR* TO THE THRONE!

OH, WELL. I GUESS A STEADY PAYCHECK *WOULD* SUPPORT MY *RESEARCH...*

25

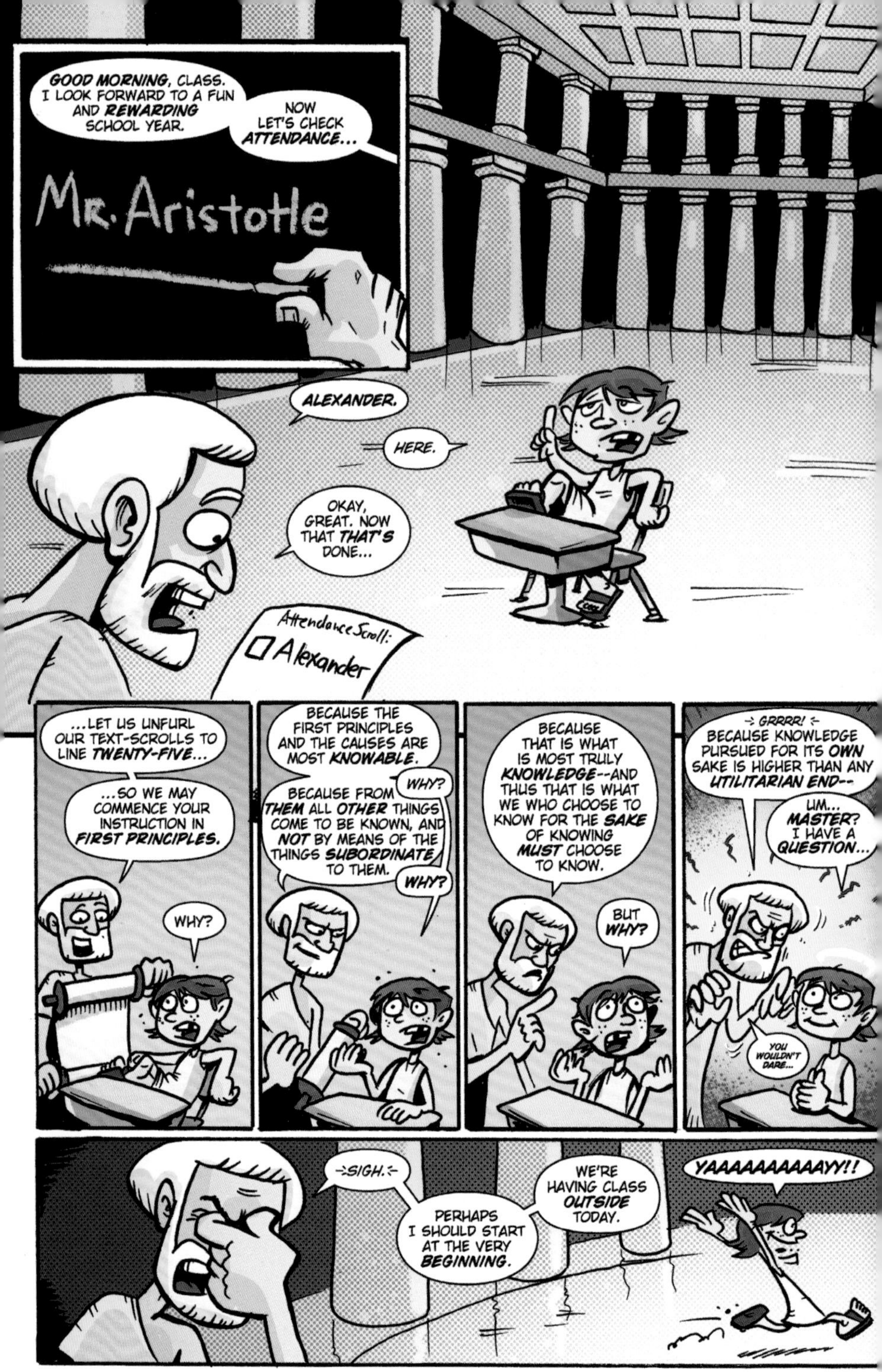
GOOD MORNING, CLASS. I LOOK FORWARD TO A FUN AND REWARDING SCHOOL YEAR.
NOW LET'S CHECK ATTENDANCE...
Mr. Aristotle
ALEXANDER.
HERE.
OKAY, GREAT. NOW THAT THAT'S DONE...
Attendance Scroll:
Alexander
...LET US UNFURL OUR TEXT-SCROLLS TO LINE TWENTY-FIVE...
...SO WE MAY COMMENCE YOUR INSTRUCTION IN FIRST PRINCIPLES.
WHY?
BECAUSE THE FIRST PRINCIPLES AND THE CAUSES ARE MOST KNOWABLE.
WHY?
BECAUSE FROM THEM ALL OTHER THINGS COME TO BE KNOWN, AND NOT BY MEANS OF THE THINGS SUBORDINATE TO THEM.
WHY?
BECAUSE THAT IS WHAT IS MOST TRULY KNOWLEDGE--AND THUS THAT IS WHAT WE WHO CHOOSE TO KNOW FOR THE SAKE OF KNOWING MUST CHOOSE TO KNOW.
BUT WHY?
GRRRR! BECAUSE KNOWLEDGE PURSUED FOR ITS OWN SAKE IS HIGHER THAN ANY UTILITARIAN END--
UM... MASTER? I HAVE A QUESTION...
YOU WOULDN'T DARE...
SIGH.
PERHAPS I SHOULD START AT THE VERY BEGINNING.
WE'RE HAVING CLASS OUTSIDE TODAY.
YAAAAAAAAAAYY!!

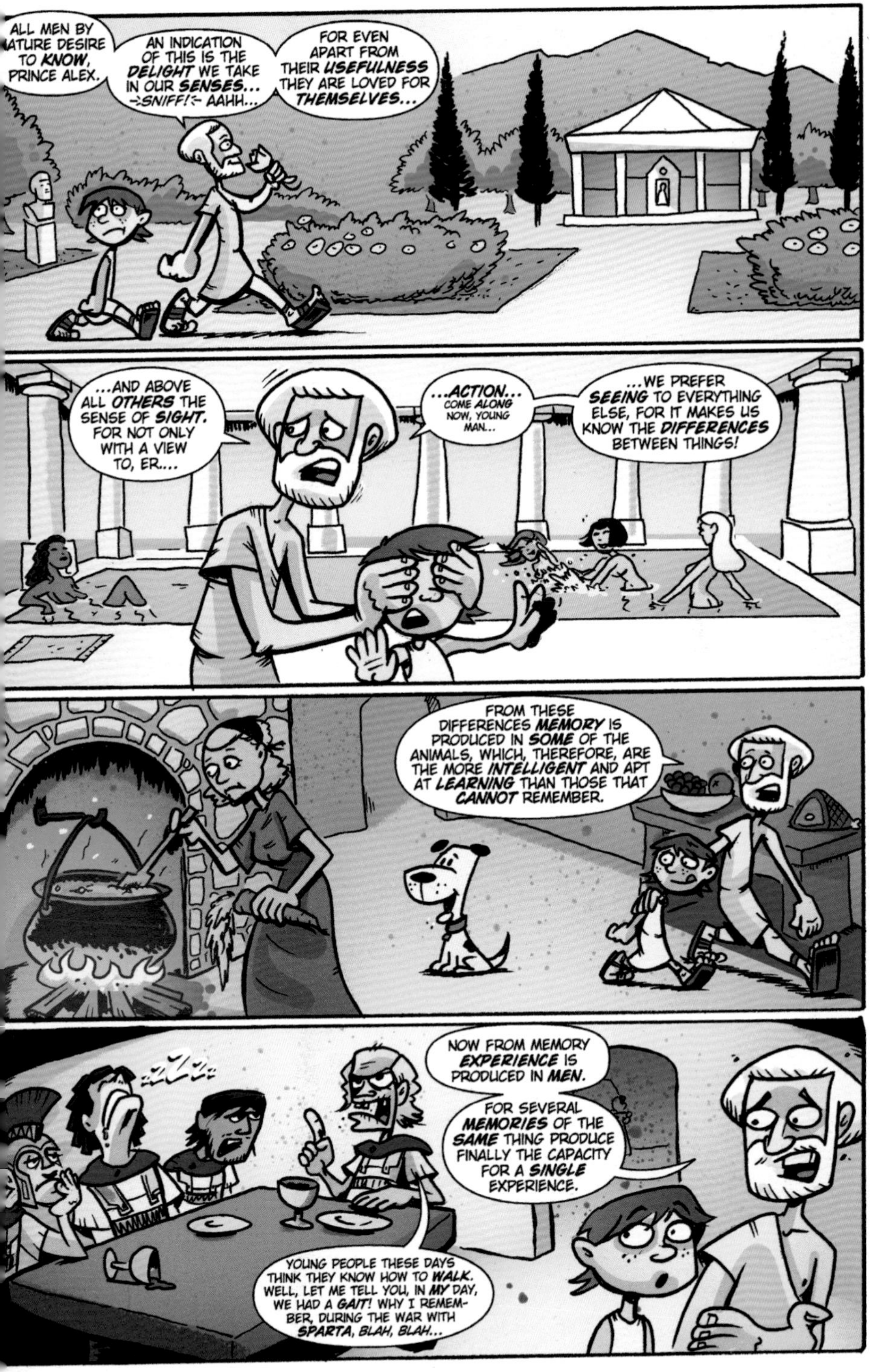
ALL MEN BY NATURE DESIRE TO KNOW, PRINCE ALEX.
AN INDICATION OF THIS IS THE DELIGHT WE TAKE IN OUR SENSES... ~SNIFF!~ AAHH...
FOR EVEN APART FROM THEIR USEFULNESS THEY ARE LOVED FOR THEMSELVES...
...AND ABOVE ALL OTHERS THE SENSE OF SIGHT. FOR NOT ONLY WITH A VIEW TO, ER....
...ACTION... COME ALONG NOW, YOUNG MAN...
...WE PREFER SEEING TO EVERYTHING ELSE, FOR IT MAKES US KNOW THE DIFFERENCES BETWEEN THINGS!
FROM THESE DIFFERENCES MEMORY IS PRODUCED IN SOME OF THE ANIMALS, WHICH, THEREFORE, ARE THE MORE INTELLIGENT AND APT AT LEARNING THAN THOSE THAT CANNOT REMEMBER.
ZZZ
NOW FROM MEMORY EXPERIENCE IS PRODUCED IN MEN.
FOR SEVERAL MEMORIES OF THE SAME THING PRODUCE FINALLY THE CAPACITY FOR A SINGLE EXPERIENCE.
YOUNG PEOPLE THESE DAYS THINK THEY KNOW HOW TO WALK. WELL, LET ME TELL YOU, IN MY DAY, WE HAD A GAIT! WHY I REMEMBER, DURING THE WAR WITH SPARTA, BLAH, BLAH...

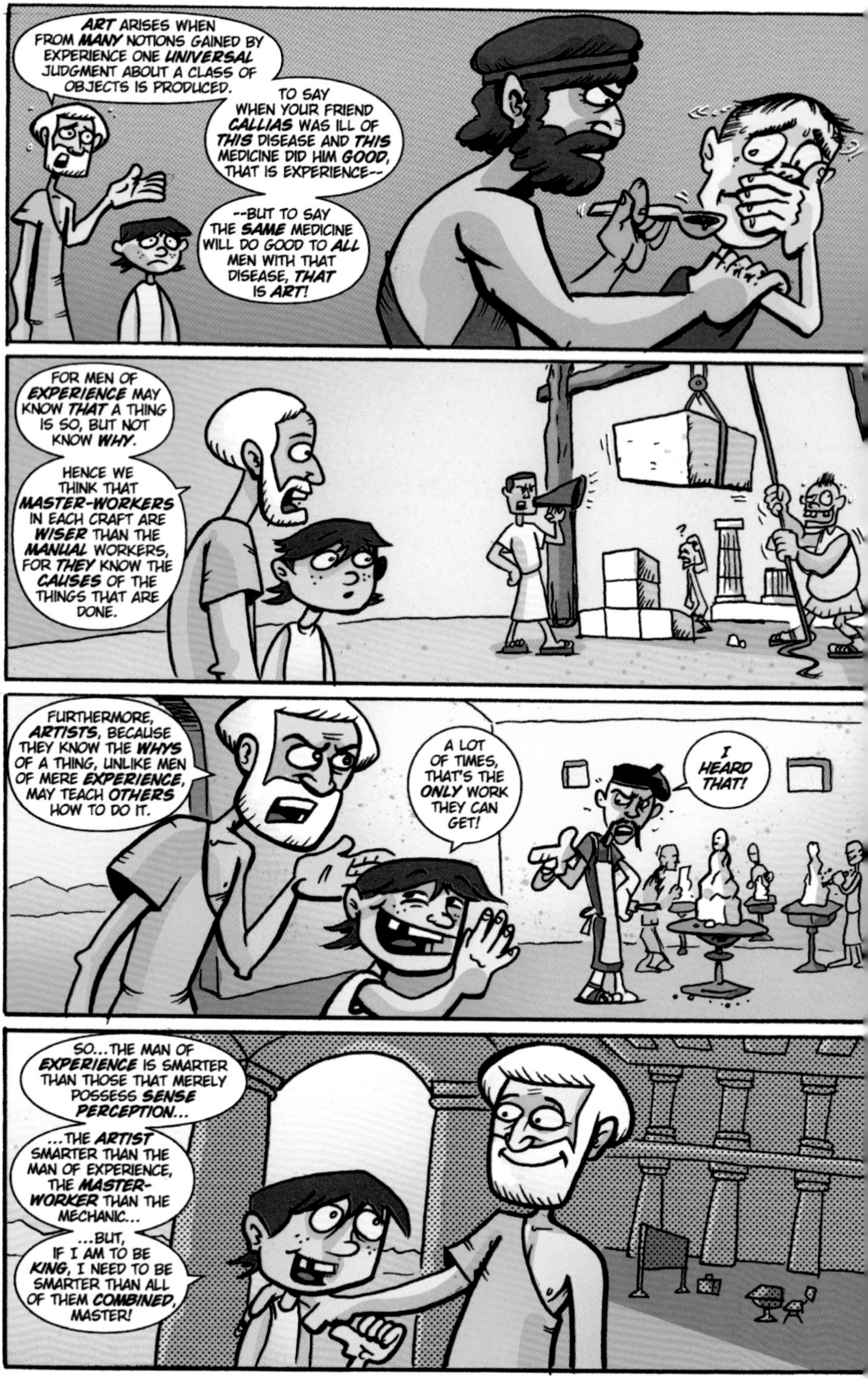
ART ARISES WHEN FROM MANY NOTIONS GAINED BY EXPERIENCE ONE UNIVERSAL JUDGMENT ABOUT A CLASS OF OBJECTS IS PRODUCED.
TO SAY WHEN YOUR FRIEND CALLIAS WAS ILL OF THIS DISEASE AND THIS MEDICINE DID HIM GOOD, THAT IS EXPERIENCE--
--BUT TO SAY THE SAME MEDICINE WILL DO GOOD TO ALL MEN WITH THAT DISEASE, THAT IS ART!
FOR MEN OF EXPERIENCE MAY KNOW THAT A THING IS SO, BUT NOT KNOW WHY.
HENCE WE THINK THAT MASTER-WORKERS IN EACH CRAFT ARE WISER THAN THE MANUAL WORKERS, FOR THEY KNOW THE CAUSES OF THE THINGS THAT ARE DONE.
FURTHERMORE, ARTISTS, BECAUSE THEY KNOW THE WHYS OF A THING, UNLIKE MEN OF MERE EXPERIENCE, MAY TEACH OTHERS HOW TO DO IT.
A LOT OF TIMES, THAT'S THE ONLY WORK THEY CAN GET!
I HEARD THAT!
SO...THE MAN OF EXPERIENCE IS SMARTER THAN THOSE THAT MERELY POSSESS SENSE PERCEPTION...
...THE ARTIST SMARTER THAN THE MAN OF EXPERIENCE, THE MASTER-WORKER THAN THE MECHANIC...
...BUT, IF I AM TO BE KING, I NEED TO BE SMARTER THAN ALL OF THEM COMBINED, MASTER!

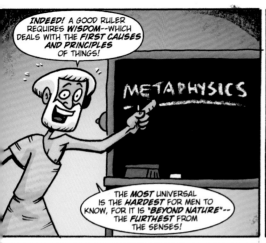

INDEED! A GOOD RULER REQUIRES *WISDOM*--WHICH DEALS WITH THE *FIRST CAUSES AND PRINCIPLES* OF THINGS!

METAPHYSICS

THE *MOST* UNIVERSAL IS THE *HARDEST* FOR MEN TO KNOW, FOR IT IS *"BEYOND NATURE"*-- THE *FURTHEST* FROM THE SENSES!

BUT THROUGH MY EXHAUSTIVE OBSERVATIONS OF THE WORKINGS OF NATURE AND MAN *ALIKE*, I HAVE CLASSIFIED THESE CAUSES INTO *FOUR* CATEGORIES!

LET'S SEE... I KNOW I HAVE THE LIST HERE *SOMEWHERE...*

WELL...I *DO* REMEMBER THAT *ONE* TYPE OF CAUSE IS THE *MATERIAL* ONE--WHAT SMALLER PARTS, OR *INGREDIENTS,* GO INTO THE WHOLE TO MAKE IT *EXIST?*

GREEK FIRE: SULFUR, PETROLEUM, PHOSPHORUS, SALTPETER!

OIL

OH, YES, AND THEN THERE'S THE *FORMAL* CAUSE--THE *DEFINITION* OR *PATTERN* THE THING FITS INTO.

LIKE... *"PRACTICAL JOKES?"* ~SNICKER!~

OIL

YES, EXACTLY! AND THEN THE *EFFICIENT* CAUSE WOULD BE THE *INCITING INCIDENT* THAT BRINGS THE THING *INTO* BEING--

SUCH AS THE *SPARK* THAT IGNITES THE *FLAMES?*

EXCELLENT, PRINCE ALEX, EXCEL-- *AH, HERE* ARE MY NOTES!

OF COURSE! THE FOURTH CAUSE IS THE *FINAL* ONE--FOR WHAT *END* DOES A THING EXIST?

~SNIFF, SNIFF...~

AAAGGH!!

IN THE CASE OF A *HOTFOOT*... BECAUSE IT'S *FREAKIN' HILARIOUS!* HA HA!!

GRRRRR!! JUST AS IN *REGULAR* PHYSICS, THE BASIS OF ALL *META*PHYSICS IS *MOTION*--

--FOR *CHANGE* ("*KINESIS*") IS THE ONLY *CONSTANT* IN NATURE!

AND THE MOST *COMMON* FORM OF CHANGE-- THE ONE *NECESSARY* TO EXISTENCE--

--IS WHEN BEINGS MOVE FROM A *POTENTIAL* STATE--

--SUCH AS AN ACORN IS A *POTENTIAL* TREE, OR A PILE OF LUMBER & BRICKS IS A *POTENTIAL* HOUSE--

--OR ME *PREPARING* TO WRING YOUR NECK--

--TO AN *ACTUAL* STATE!

SNOT-- NOSED--LITTLE-- ROYAL--PUNK! SET ME ON FIRE, WILLYA--

=GAK!=

=CHOKE!=

ARISTOTLE! HOW GOES THE BOY'S FIRST DAY OF *STUDY?*

KING PHILIP! AH... WELL...

GASP! WHEEZE!

30

W-WE WERE JUST DISCUSSING HOW *ACTUALITY* IS THE —*GULP*—...

...*END* (TELOS) OF POTENTIALITY!

A-ANOTHER WAY OF PUTTING IT IS THAT *SUBSTANCE,* OR PURE MATTER, IS POTENTIAL *BEING,* BUT IS G-GIVEN *FORM* IN ACTUALITY—

YEESH! TOO *EGGHEAD* FOR ME!

I HAVE *SUBJECTS* THAT NEED *OPPRESSING!*

THANKS FOR *DROPPING BY,* SIRE...

—*HEH.*— SORRY.

SO YOU'RE THE *RESTLESS* TYPE, EH?

NEED AN *ACTIVITY* WITH WHICH TO OCCUPY YOUR TIME?

LUCKY FOR YOU, I HAVE *JUST THE THING!*

WE HAVE *TRUE* KNOWLEDGE ONLY WHEN WE THINK WE KNOW THE *CAUSE* ON WHICH A FACT DEPENDS, AS THE CAUSE OF *THAT* FACT AND *NO* OTHER, AND FURTHER, THAT THE FACT COULD *NOT* BE OTHER THAN *IT IS.*

AND WE *CONNECT* CAUSES TO FACTS THROUGH A LITTLE *INVENTION* OF MINE I CALL...

LOGIC!

OH. GOODY.

BLOCKS.

31

THE FUNDAMENTAL CONSTRUCTION OF LOGIC IS THE **SYLLOGISM**...

...A DISCOURSE IN WHICH CERTAIN THINGS BEING STATED...

...SOMETHING **OTHER** THAN WHAT IS STATED FOLLOWS **OF NECESSITY** FROM THEIR **BEING SO.**

IN **OTHER** WORDS:

IF A IS PREDICATED OF ALL B AND B IS PREDICATED OF ALL C, THEN A IS NECESSARILY PREDICATED OF ALL OF C!

OKAY...OR, IN OTHER, MORE **UNDERSTANDABLE** WORDS...

A
MAJOR PREMISE

"ALL MEN ARE MORTAL."

B
MINOR PREMISE

CENSORED

"SOCRATES IS A MAN."

C
CONCLUSION

CRAP.

"THEREFORE, SOCRATES IS MORTAL."

BY **ZEUS**, ALEX, I THINK YOU'VE **GOT** IT!

YEARS PASSED THIS WAY, BUT ALEXANDER'S SCHOOLING FINALLY CAME TO AN **ABRUPT END** UPON HIS FATHER'S **ASSASSINATION** IN 336 B.C., NECESSITATING THE PRINCE'S **CORONATION**.

MY ARMIES AND I MARCH EAST TO **PERSIA**, MASTER. WOULD YOU COME **WITH** ME, SO I MIGHT CONTINUE TO BENEFIT FROM YOUR WISE COUNSEL?

THANK YOU, ALE--

YOUR **MAJESTY**, I MEAN! -:HEH!:- BUT **NO**...

"...I HAVE RESOLVED TO RETURN TO **ATHENS**...AND USE THE MONEY I EARNED **HERE** TO BUY LAND FOR MY **OWN** SCHOOL!"

SOCRATES **HIMSELF** CAME TO THINK UNDER THESE GROVES--SACRED AS THEY ARE TO APOLLO LYCEUS, THE **LIGHT-GIVER**!

OOH! GOOD **KARMA**! I'LL **TAKE** IT!

ARISTOTLE'S **LYCEUM** OPENED AROUND 334 B.C. HIS UNUSUAL TEACHING METHOD INVOLVED WALKING AROUND A **PERIPATOS**, OR COVERED WALK...SO HIS SCHOOL WAS CALLED **"PERIPATETIC."**

MASTER, YOU'VE RECEIVED A LETTER FROM YOUR FORMER **PUPIL**, THE KING OF **MACEDON**!

READ IT TO ME, WILL YOU?

Dear Master,

Having a **smashing time** conquering Asia Minor. And I do mean that **literally**! Ha, ha!

But **seriously**, in my campaigns I have come across many fascinating **specimens** that will help you in your **research**. I will be sending them to you shortly.

Whoops— The ground is **shaking**, so that must mean enemy **war elephants** are on their way! No rest for the **wicked**!

Hope the Lyceum is going well and I will write again soon.

XOXOXOXOX ALEX.

BY 323 B.C., **ALEXANDER THE GREAT** HAD ESTABLISHED THE LARGEST EMPIRE IN **HISTORY**-- ONE THAT STRETCHED FROM EGYPT TO INDIA AND INCLUDED THE CITY-STATE OF **ATHENS** HERSELF!

WHERE IS THAT SHIPMENT OF **SLIDE RULES** I ORDERED? I CAN'T TEACH **GYM** WITHOUT THEM!!

I-I'M **SORRY**, SPEUSIPPUS, BUT THE ACADEMY IS NEAR **BROKE**! ENROLLMENT IS DOWN **EIGHTY PERCENT** THIS YEAR!

WHAT? HOW IS THAT **POSSIBLE?** WHERE COULD ALL OUR STUDENTS BE **GOING**-?

GAHHH!!

THE LYCEUM: We made Alexander **GREAT!**

SO **THIS** IS THE LYCEUM, EH?

TO: MASTER FROM: ALEX

WELL, I COULD BE THE GREATEST GENIUS OF THE ANCIENTS TOO, IF I HAD THE RULER OF THE **KNOWN WORLD** ON MY **ALUMNI MAILING LIST**...GRUMBLE, MUMBLE...

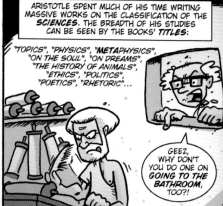

ARISTOTLE SPENT MUCH OF HIS TIME WRITING MASSIVE WORKS ON THE CLASSIFICATION OF THE **SCIENCES**. THE BREADTH OF HIS STUDIES CAN BE SEEN BY THE BOOKS' **TITLES**:

"TOPICS", "PHYSICS", "**META**PHYSICS", "ON THE SOUL", "ON DREAMS", "THE HISTORY OF ANIMALS", "ETHICS", "POLITICS", "POETICS", "RHETORIC"...

GEEZ, WHY DON'T YOU DO ONE ON **GOING TO THE BATHROOM**, TOO?!

34

DONE!

GRRR!!

ALEXANDER DIED AFTER A NIGHT OF HEAVY *BOOZING* -- AND POSSIBLY FROM A TROPICAL DISEASE LIKE *MALARIA* -- ON JUNE 11, 323 B.C., IN *BABYLON*. WHEN ASKED WHO SHOULD *SUCCEED* HIM, HE REPLIED:

THE *STRONGEST!*

WHILE HIS GENERALS BATTLED OVER HIS *CROWN*, ALEXANDER'S EMPIRE SWIFTLY *CRUMBLED*.

~*TSK!*~ POOR *ALEX!* HE WAS ONLY *THIRTY-THREE*.

WE CAN ONLY HOPE, WITH HIM *GONE*, THAT THE POLITICAL SITUATION *HERE* DOESN'T DEGENERATE TOO *QUICKLY*--

WE SHALL *PURGE* ATHENS OF ALEXANDER'S TYRANNY...

...AND HIS MACEDONIAN *PUPPETS!*

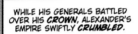
LYCEUM

GAAHH!!

LIKE SOCRATES *BEFORE* HIM, ARISTOTLE WAS CHARGED WITH *"IMPIETY"*, OBLIGING HIM TO FLEE THE CITY...

ATHENS CITY LIMITS

...LEST THE ATHENIANS SIN AGAINST PHILOSOPHY *TWICE!**

*ACTUAL QUOTE!

35

Diogenes the Cynic!

The root of **"cynic"** is the Greek *kunikos*, or *"doglike."*

How this philosopher from Sinope earned that appellation is not hard to **figure out...**

Diogenes believed that **nature**, not social **convention**, showed the way to a virtuous life.

Unlike animals, the only leash a **wise** man needs to police his action and expression is his own **reason!**

The Cynics held **abstract thinking** in contempt—any philosophy with **value** had to be **lived.**

And the key to good living is **simplicity**—Diogenes liberated himself from the ownership of any **possessions.**

"He has the **most** who is most content with the **least!**"

Observing a **mouse** needed no real shelter, he lived in a busted *pithos*, or **tub!**

Human customs **confuse** nature's path, so Diogenes **ridiculed** tradition by continuously **flaunting** his repeated violations of the same...

...doing **everything** in public: including drinking, eating (etiquette **no-nos** in ancient Athens) and even **masturbating** in the marketplace!

Ugh! He's got no more **shame** than a **stray dog!**

He also knew how to **bark** at human folly...

Please, Zeus, let me become **rich** and **famous...**

?

Woof! Woof!

How **dare** you **insult** the gods asking for things you **think** will make you happy...

...when they have **already** given you everything you **need** for happiness?

You may oppose bad luck with **courage**, bad company with **nature**, and bad feelings with **reason!**

PLATO, AN ABSTRACT THINKER WHO CURRIED POLITICAL FAVOR, WAS DIOGENES' FAVORITE CHEW TOY.

WE MAY DEFINE A *HUMAN BEING* AS AN ANIMAL WHO IS *BIPEDAL* AND *FEATHERLESS*.

I RAN INTO THIS *HUMAN BEING* OUTSIDE, WISE PLATO...

...I *WONDER*, COULD HE PASS THE *ENTRANCE EXAM* FOR YOUR ACADEMY?

NOT EVEN *ALEXANDER THE GREAT* WAS SAFE FROM THE CYNIC'S BITE...

MANY SAY YOU ARE THE *WISEST* MAN IN ALL OF ATHENS, DIOGENES-- EVEN MORESO THAN *MY* TEACHER, ARISTOTLE!

IF YOU PROVIDE ME WITH SOME *USEFUL* INSIGHT, I WILL GRANT YOU *ANY* BOON YOU ASK!

WHAT IS YOUR GREATEST *DESIRE* AT THE PRESENT TIME, MAJESTY?

TO CONQUER ALL OF *GREECE*!

AND *THEN* WHAT SHALL YOU DO?

THEN I PLAN TO MARCH ON *TURKEY*!

AND *THEN* WHAT?

THEN THE *REST* OF THE KNOWN WORLD WILL FALL BEFORE MY ARMIES!

THAT'S NICE. *THEN*?

ER ... WELL ... I SUPPOSE AFTER *THAT* I WILL RELAX AND *ENJOY* MYSELF!

THEN MY PIECE OF WISDOM FOR *YOU*, YOUNG MAN...

...IS TO *SKIP* ALL THAT BOTHER AND JUST START RELAXING AND ENJOYING YOURSELF RIGHT *NOW*!

-*HEH.*- YOU *ARE* QUITE THE CLEVER ONE, DIOGENES.

WHAT *REWARD* DO YOU ASK?

JUST... COULD YOU MOVE A FEW INCHES TO THE *RIGHT*?

YOU'RE BLOCKING MY *SUN*!

PRINCIPLE #1:
A *HAPPY* AND ETERNAL BEING HAS NO TROUBLE HIMSELF AND *BRINGS* NO TROUBLE UPON ANY OTHER BEING;

HENCE HE IS *EXEMPT* FROM MOVEMENTS OF ANGER AND PARTIALITY, FOR EVERY SUCH MOVEMENT IMPLIES *WEAKNESS!*

NO ONE WAS HAPPIER TO CREATE THIS COMIC THAN FRED VAN LENTE (WRITER) AND RYAN DUNLAVEY (ARTIST)!

THUS BEGINS THE *PRINCIPLE DOCTRINES OF ACTION PHILOSOPHER #29* (341-270 BC):

EPICURUS!

PRINCIPLE #2: DEATH IS *NOTHING* TO US.

FOR WHAT HAS BEEN DISPERSED HAS NO *FEELING,* AND THAT WHICH HAS NO FEELING IS *NOTHING* TO US.

SCREW THIS! I CAN'T *SLAY* THIS CROWD!

SOME OTHER COMIC BEAT ME *TO* IT!

PRINCIPLE #3: THE LIMIT OF *PLEASURE* IS THE REMOVAL OF ALL *PAIN.*

THAT'S MORE *LIKE* IT!

V.A. HOSPITAL

HA!

HA, HA!

HA!

WHEN *PLEASURE* IS PRESENT, THERE CAN BE *NO PAIN* EITHER OF BODY OR OF MIND OR OF *BOTH* TOGETHER.

EEYYAAGGHH!!

62 seconds

PRINCIPLE #4: CONTINUOUS PAIN DOES NOT LAST **LONG** IN THE BODY...

...EVEN THAT DEGREE OF PAIN WHICH BARELY **OUTWEIGHS** PLEASURE IN THE BODY DOES NOT LAST FOR MANY DAYS TOGETHER.

62 years

~SIGH!~

PRINCIPLE #5: IT IS IMPOSSIBLE TO LIVE A **PLEASANT** LIFE WITHOUT LIVING **WISELY** AND WELL AND JUSTLY, AND IT IS IMPOSSIBLE TO LIVE **WISELY** AND WELL AND JUSTLY WITHOUT LIVING **PLEASANTLY.**

WHERE DOES ALL THE TIME GO?!

DON'T BE A LOSER

BUY MORE STUFF

$ $ $ $

WHENEVER ANY **ONE** OF THESE IS LACKING, WHEN, FOR INSTANCE, THE PERSON IS NOT ABLE TO LIVE **WISELY**, THOUGH HE LIVES WELL AND JUSTLY, IT IS **IMPOSSIBLE** FOR HIM TO LIVE A **PLEASANT** LIFE.

PRINCIPLE #8: NO PLEASURE IS IN ITSELF **EVIL**...

~SIGH!~ I'VE WASTED MY LIFE...

A-C   C-E

E-H   H-L

M   N-R

S   T-X

...BUT THE THINGS WHICH **PRODUCE** CERTAIN PLEASURES ENTAIL **TROUBLES** MANY TIMES GREATER THAN THE **PLEASURES** THEMSELVES.

PRINCIPLE #9: IF **EVERY** PLEASURE WERE MAXIMIZED AND EXISTED FOR A **LONG** TIME THROUGHOUT THE **ENTIRE** ORGANISM OR ITS MOST IMPORTANT PARTS, PLEASURES WOULD NEVER **DIFFER** FROM ONE ANOTHER.

THIS IS THE GREATEST DAY OF MY LIFE!

POP POP POP POP POP POP POP POP POP POP POP POP POP POP POP

AND THE NOBEL PRIZE FOR COMICS GOES TO...

THIS IS THE GREATEST DAY OF MY LIFE!

PRINCIPLE #10: IF THE THINGS THAT BEGET PLEASURE IN *DISSOLUTE* PERSONS DISPEL THEIR MINDS' *FEARS* ... IF, FURTHER, THEY TAUGHT THEM TO *LIMIT* THEIR DESIRES...

...WE SHOULD NEVER HAVE ANY *FAULT* TO FIND WITH THE DISSOLUTE, FOR THEY WOULD THEN BE *FILLED* WITH PLEASURES FROM EVERY SOURCE AND IN NO WAY *SUFFERING* FROM PAIN OR GRIEF, WHICH IS EVIL.

IF APPREHENSIONS ABOUT THE *HEAVENS* AND OUR FEAR LEST *DEATH* CONCERN US, AS WELL AS OUR FAILURE TO REALIZE THE *LIMITS* OF PAINS AND DESIRES, DID NOT *BOTHER* US, WE WOULD HAVE *NO NEED* OF *NATURAL SCIENCE*.

PRINCIPLE #13: THERE IS NO BENEFIT IN SECURING PROTECTION FROM *MEN* IF THINGS ABOVE AND BENEATH THE EARTH AND INDEED ALL THE LIMITLESS *UNIVERSE* ARE MADE MATTERS FOR *SUSPICION*.

PRINCIPLE #14:

THE MOST PERFECT MEANS OF SECURING *SAFETY* FROM MEN, WHICH ARISES, TO SOME EXTENT, FROM A CERTAIN POWER TO *EXPEL*, IS THE *ASSURANCE* THAT COMES FROM QUIETUDE AND *WITHDRAWAL* FROM THE WORLD.

PRINCIPLE #15:

NATURAL WEALTH IS *LIMITED* AND *EASILY* OBTAINED;

THE *RICHES* OF *IDLE FANCIES* GO ON *FOREVER.*

PRINCIPLE #17:

THE *JUST* PERSON IS MOST *FREE* OF ANXIETY, WHILE THE *UNJUST* PERSON IS *FULL* OF IT.

PRINCIPLE #21: HE WHO UNDERSTANDS THE *LIMITS* OF LIFE KNOWS HOW *EASY* IT IS TO PROCURE *ENOUGH* TO REMOVE THE PAIN OF WANT AND MAKE THE *WHOLE* OF LIFE COMPLETE AND *PERFECT.*

HENCE HE HAS NO LONGER ANY *NEED* OF THINGS THAT ARE NOT TO BE WON SAVE BY LABOR AND CONFLICT.

PRINCIPLE #22: WE MUST TAKE INTO ACCOUNT ALL THE EVIDENCE OF *CLEAR PERCEPTION*, TO WHICH WE REFER OUR OPINIONS. OTHERWISE, EVERYTHING WILL BE FILLED WITH *CONFUSION* AND INDECISION.

PRINCIPLE #23: IF YOU *FIGHT* AGAINST ALL YOUR SENSATIONS, YOU WILL BE UNABLE TO FORM A STANDARD FOR JUDGING EVEN WHICH OF THEM YOU JUDGE TO BE *FALSE.*

PRINCIPLE #26:

THOSE DESIRES THAT DO NOT LEAD TO *PAIN* IF THEY ARE UNFULFILLED ARE *UNNECESSARY*.

HMMM...

THEY INVOLVE A *LONGING* THAT IS EASILY *DISPELLED*, WHENEVER IT IS *DIFFICULT* TO FULFILL THE DESIRES OR THEY APPEAR LIKELY TO LEAD TO *HARM*.

PRINCIPLE #27:

OF ALL THE MEANS THAT ARE PROCURED BY *WISDOM* TO ENSURE HAPPINESS *THROUGHOUT* THE WHOLE OF LIFE, BY FAR THE *MOST* IMPORTANT...

...IS *FRIENDSHIP*.

PRINCIPLE #29: OF OUR DESIRES SOME ARE *NATURAL* AND *NECESSARY*; OTHERS ARE NATURAL, BUT *NOT* NECESSARY; OTHERS, AGAIN, ARE NEITHER NATURAL *NOR* NECESSARY, BUT ARE DUE TO ILLUSORY *OPINION*.

You Want IT! You Need IT! Get IT before your friends! IT is awesome!

$ $ $

PRINCIPLE #32:

THOSE ANIMALS THAT ARE *INCAPABLE* OF MAKING *COVENANTS* WITH ONE ANOTHER, TO THE END THAT THEY MAY NEITHER INFLICT NOR SUFFER HARM, ARE *WITHOUT* EITHER JUSTICE OR INJUSTICE.

MY GOD NO!

I'VE INVENTED LAWYERS!

PRINCIPLE #34: INJUSTICE IS NOT IN *ITSELF* AN EVIL, BUT ONLY IN ITS *CONSEQUENCE, VIZ.* THE *TERROR* WHICH IS EXCITED BY APPREHENSION THAT THOSE APPOINTED TO PUNISH SUCH OFFENSES WILL *DISCOVER* THE INJUSTICE.

THUMP THUMP THUMP THUMP

PRINCIPLE #35: IT IS IMPOSSIBLE FOR THE PERSON WHO SECRETLY VIOLATES ANY ARTICLE OF THE SOCIAL COMPACT TO FEEL CONFIDENT THAT HE WILL REMAIN *UNDISCOVERED*, EVEN IF HE HAS ALREADY ESCAPED TEN THOUSAND TIMES; FOR RIGHT ON TO THE *END* OF HIS LIFE HE IS NEVER SURE HE WILL NOT BE *DETECTED*.

PRINCIPLE #40: THOSE WHO WERE BEST ABLE TO PROVIDE THEMSELVES WITH THE MEANS OF *SECURITY* AGAINST THEIR NEIGHBORS, BEING THUS IN POSSES-SION OF THE SUREST GUARANTEE, PASSED THE MOST *AGREEABLE* LIFE IN EACH OTHER'S SOCIETY;

AND THEIR ENJOYMENT OF THE FULLEST INTIMACY WAS SUCH THAT, IF ONE OF THEM *DIED* BEFORE HIS TIME, THE SURVIVORS DID *NOT* MOURN HIS DEATH AS IF IT CALLED FOR *SYMPATHY*.

POPPOPPOP POPPOPPOP POPPOPPOP

YEAH, YEAH, WE GET IT: BUBBLE WRAP IS PLEASURABLE.

CAN WE HURRY THIS UP?! I GOTTA BE IN SRI LANKA BY FIVE...

43

EPICTETUS THE STOIC!

THIS PHILOSOPHER'S REAL NAME REMAINS *UNKNOWN* -- "EPICTETUS" SIMPLY MEANS *"SLAVE"*.

HIS ROMAN MASTER ALLOWED HIM TO BE TUTORED IN A SCHOOL OF THOUGHT DEVELOPED BY *ZENO OF CITIUM*, A CITY ON THE SOUTHEAST COAST OF WHAT IS NOW *CYPRUS*.

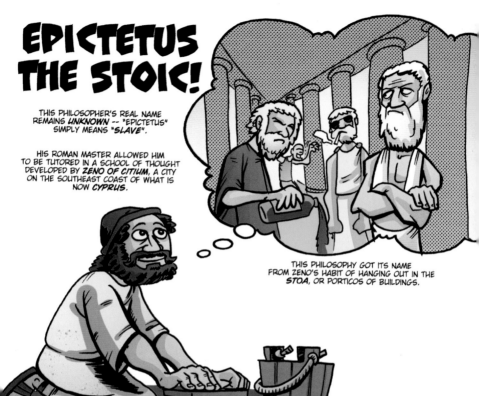

THIS PHILOSOPHY GOT ITS NAME FROM ZENO'S HABIT OF HANGING OUT IN THE *STOA*, OR PORTICOS OF BUILDINGS.

DIOGENES LAËRTIUS WRITES THAT THE STOICS THOUGHT OF PHILOSOPHY LIKE AN *EGG*:

"THE SHELL IS *LOGIC*, NEXT COMES THE WHITE, *ETHICS*, AND THE YOLK IN THE CENTER IS *PHYSICS*."

ALL STOIC *PHYSICAL* THEORY RETURNS TO THE IDEA THAT GOD IS *IN ALL THINGS*.

THERE ARE TWO PRINCIPLES FOR THE UNIVERSE: THE *ACTIVE* AND THE *PASSIVE*.

MATTER IS THE *PASSIVE* FORM OF GOD AND GOD IS THE *ACTIVE* FORM OF *MATTER*.

THE ROMAN STOIC *SENECA* WROTE:

WHY SHOULD YOU NOT BELIEVE THAT SOMETHING OF *DIVINITY* EXISTS IN ONE WHO IS PART OF *GOD*?

THE WHOLE UNIVERSE THAT CONTAINS US IS ONE, AND IS *GOD*; WE ARE HIS ASSOCIATES AND HIS *MEMBERS*.

GOD

ZENO HIMSELF USES *THIS* ANALOGY:

"IF *PLANE TREES* BORE *LYRES* RESOUNDING MELODIOUSLY, YOU WOULD ALSO NATURALLY THINK THAT *MUSIC* EXISTED IN *PLANE TREES*."

"WHY, THEREFORE, IS THE *WORLD* NOT CONSIDERED *ANIMATE* AND INTELLIGENT, WHEN IT PRODUCES FROM *ITSELF* ANIMATE AND INTELLIGENT *BEINGS*?"

THEREFORE *NOTHING*, AS PLUTARCH SAYS, "EITHER RESTS OR IS MOVED OTHERWISE THAN ACCORDING TO THE REASON OF *GOD*, WHICH IS THE SAME THING AS *FATE*."

LITTLE WONDER THAT SUCH A *FATALISTIC* OUTLOOK ATTRACTED ADHERENTS AMONG *SLAVES*...

...BUT OUR NAMELESS HERO WANTED TO *CONTINUE* TO PREACH STOICISM IN ROME EVEN *AFTER* HE BOUGHT HIS *FREEDOM*!

UNFORTUNATELY FOR *HIM*, THE PARANOID EMPEROR *DOMITIAN* *EXILED* ALL PHILOSOPHERS FROM THE IMPERIAL CAPITAL IN A.D. 94.

AND *STAY OUT*!

EPICTETUS WOUND UP IN GREECE, SPECIFICALLY *EPIRUS*, WHERE HIS TEACHINGS REALLY BEGAN TO *CATCH ON*.

AFTER HE DIED AROUND 127, HIS STUDENT *FLAVIUS ARRIAN* ASSEMBLED HIS TEACHINGS INTO EIGHT *DISCOURSES*--

--THE *ETHICAL* PARTS OF WHICH HE CONDENSED INTO THE *ENCHIRIDION (MANUAL)*, WHICH FAMOUSLY BEGINS:

OF ALL EXISTING THINGS, SOME ARE *IN* OUR POWER, AND OTHERS ARE *NOT* IN OUR POWER.

IN OUR POWER ARE THOUGHT, IMPULSE, WILL TO *GET* AND WILL TO *AVOID*...

THINGS IN OUR POWER ARE BY NATURE *FREE*, UNHINDERED, UNTRAMMELED.

...IN A WORD, EVERYTHING WHICH *IS* OUR OWN DOING.

THINGS *NOT* IN OUR POWER INCLUDE THE BODY, PROPERTY, REPUTATION, OFFICE...

...IN A WORD, EVERYTHING WHICH IS *NOT* OUR OWN DOING.

THINGS *NOT* IN OUR POWER ARE WEAK, SERVILE, SUBJECT TO HINDRANCE, DEPENDENT ON OTHERS.

REMEMBER THEN THAT IF YOU IMAGINE WHAT IS NATURALLY *SLAVISH* IS FREE, AND WHAT IS NATURALLY ANOTHER'S IS *YOUR OWN*...

...YOU WILL BE *HAMPERED*, YOU WILL MOURN, YOU WILL BE PUT TO *CONFUSION*, YOU WILL BLAME GODS AND MEN.

BUT IF YOU THINK THAT ONLY YOUR OWN BELONGS TO YOU, AND THAT WHAT IS ANOTHER'S IS INDEED ANOTHER'S....

NO ONE WILL HARM YOU, YOU WILL HAVE NO ENEMY, FOR NO HARM CAN *TOUCH* YOU.

46

AIMING THEN AT THESE *LOFTY MATTERS*, YOU MUST REMEMBER THAT TO *ATTAIN* THEM REQUIRES MORE THAN *ORDINARY* EFFORT.

YOU WILL HAVE TO GIVE UP SOME THINGS ENTIRELY, AND PUT OTHERS *OFF* FOR THE MOMENT.

AND IF YOU WOULD HAVE STATUS AND WEALTH, YOU MAY *FAIL* TO GET THEM, JUST BECAUSE YOUR DESIRE IS SET ON THE *FORMER*...

...AND YOU WILL *CERTAINLY* FAIL TO ATTAIN THOSE THINGS WHICH ALONE BRING FREEDOM AND *HAPPINESS*.

MAKE IT YOUR STUDY THEN TO CONFRONT *EVERY* HARSH IMPRESSION WITH THE WORDS:

YOU ARE BUT AN *IMPRESSION*, AND NOT AT ALL WHAT YOU *SEEM TO BE*.

THEN *TEST IT* BY THOSE RULES THAT YOU POSSESS; AND FIRST BY *THIS*:

ARE YOU CONCERNED WITH WHAT *IS* IN MY POWER OR WITH WHAT IS *NOT* IN MY POWER?

AND IF IT IS CONCERNED WITH WHAT IS *NOT* IN YOUR POWER...

I HAVE NO CONTROL OVER WHAT *EVIL PEOPLE* MIGHT DO!

...BE READY WITH THE ANSWER THAT IT IS *NOTHING* TO YOU.

CURSES! LOST *ANOTHER* ONE!

WHAT TROUBLES MEN ARE NOT *THINGS*, BUT RATHER THE JUDGMENTS THEY MAKE *ABOUT* THINGS.

FOR EXAMPLE, *DEATH* HAS NOTHING ABOUT IT TO BE FEARED, OR ELSE IT WOULD HAVE APPEARED FEARFUL TO SOCRATES.

BUT THE *JUDGMENT* THAT DEATH HAS SOMETHING FEARFUL ABOUT IT--*THAT* IS WHAT IS FEARFUL.

47

REMEMBER THAT YOU SHOULD BEHAVE IN LIFE AS AT A *BANQUET.*

WHEN THE DISH THAT IS BEING PASSED AROUND COMES TO YOU, REACH OUT YOUR HAND AND TAKE IT WITH DISCRETION.

IF IT HAS *NOT* YET ARRIVED, DO NOT *ANTICIPATE* IT FROM AFAR WITH YOUR DESIRES -- *WAIT* UNTIL IT REACHES YOU.

DO THE SAME WITH STATUS, LOVE, AND *MONEY,* AND YOU WILL BE WORTHY TO SIT ONE DAY AT THE TABLE OF THE *GODS.*

REMEMBER THAT YOU ARE AN *ACTOR* OF A ROLE THAT THE AUTHOR WANTED A *CERTAIN* WAY;

SHORT, IF HE WANTED IT SHORT;

LONG, IF HE WANTED IT LONG;

IT IS UP TO YOU TO PLAY *WELL* THE CHARACTER THAT IS *GIVEN* TO YOU.

BUT *CHOOSING* IT--

THAT IS UP TO SOMEONE *ELSE.*

SCRIPT

IF YOU TRY TO ACT A PART *BEYOND* YOUR POWERS, YOU NOT ONLY *DISGRACE* YOURSELF WITH IT...

...BUT YOU *NEGLECT* THE PART WHICH YOU *COULD* HAVE FILLED WITH *SUCCESS.*

ERROR

NEVER SAY OF ANYTHING, *"I LOST IT",* BUT SAY, *"I GAVE IT BACK."*

RETURNS

HAS YOUR ESTATE BEEN *TAKEN* FROM YOU? IT WAS GIVEN *BACK.*

HAS YOUR SON *DIED?* WAS NOT THIS ALSO *GIVEN BACK?*

BUT YOU SAY, *"HE WHO TOOK IT FROM ME IS WICKED."*

WHAT DOES IT MATTER TO YOU THROUGH *WHOM* THE GIVER ASKED IT BACK? AS LONG AS GOD GIVES IT TO YOU, TAKE CARE OF IT, BUT NOT AS YOUR *OWN;* TREAT IT AS TRAVELERS TREAT AN *INN.*

48

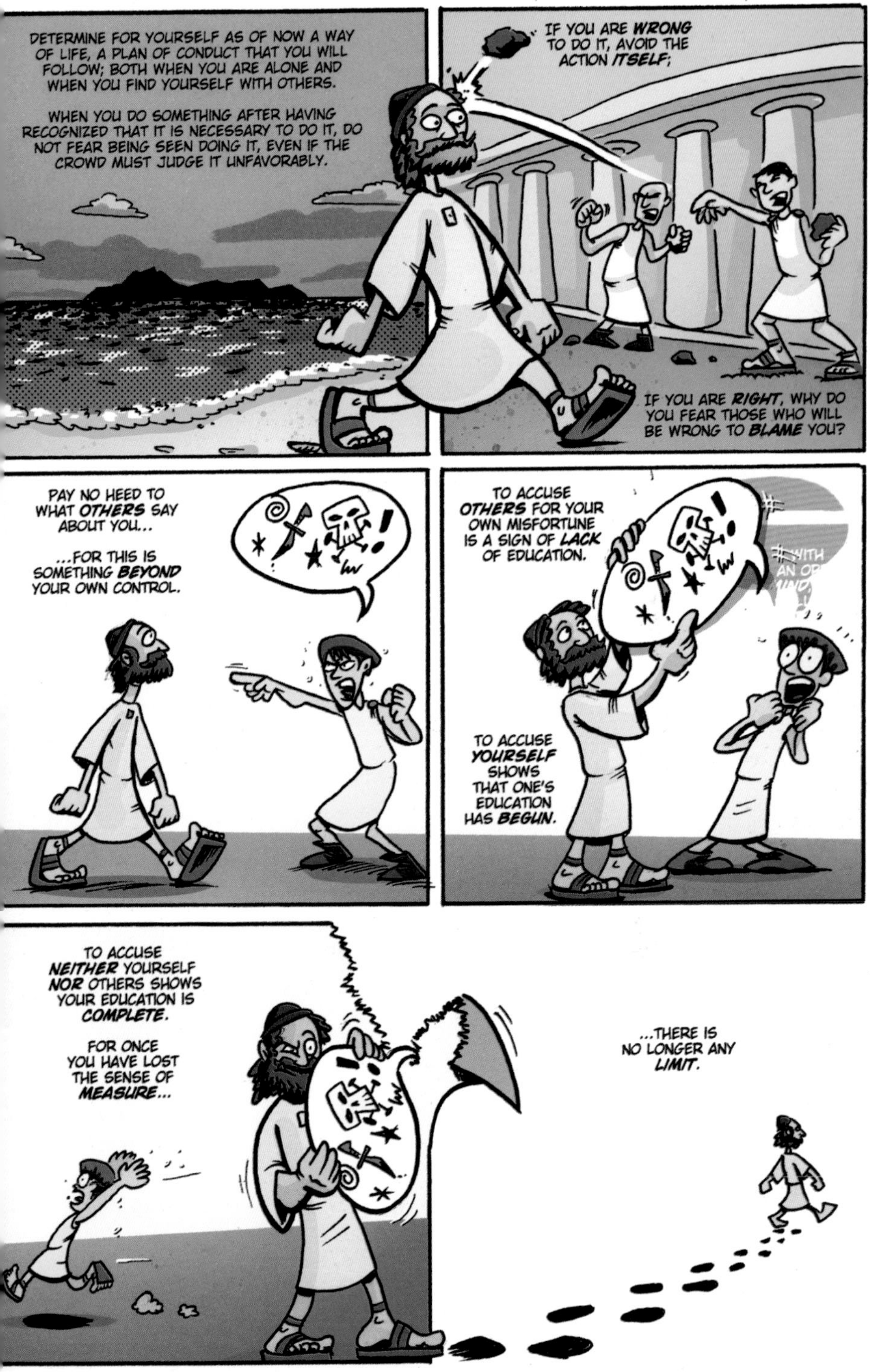
DETERMINE FOR YOURSELF AS OF NOW A WAY OF LIFE, A PLAN OF CONDUCT THAT YOU WILL FOLLOW; BOTH WHEN YOU ARE ALONE AND WHEN YOU FIND YOURSELF WITH OTHERS.
WHEN YOU DO SOMETHING AFTER HAVING RECOGNIZED THAT IT IS NECESSARY TO DO IT, DO NOT FEAR BEING SEEN DOING IT, EVEN IF THE CROWD MUST JUDGE IT UNFAVORABLY.
IF YOU ARE **WRONG** TO DO IT, AVOID THE ACTION **ITSELF**;
IF YOU ARE **RIGHT**, WHY DO YOU FEAR THOSE WHO WILL BE WRONG TO **BLAME** YOU?
PAY NO HEED TO WHAT **OTHERS** SAY ABOUT YOU...
...FOR THIS IS SOMETHING **BEYOND** YOUR OWN CONTROL.
TO ACCUSE **OTHERS** FOR YOUR OWN MISFORTUNE IS A SIGN OF **LACK** OF EDUCATION.
TO ACCUSE **YOURSELF** SHOWS THAT ONE'S EDUCATION HAS **BEGUN**.
TO ACCUSE **NEITHER** YOURSELF **NOR** OTHERS SHOWS YOUR EDUCATION IS **COMPLETE**.
FOR ONCE YOU HAVE LOST THE SENSE OF **MEASURE**...
...THERE IS NO LONGER ANY **LIMIT**.

LAO  TZU

: "MM MMOW MEH MAH ME MAMMH ME MAH ME MEMER-NAL MOW."

: "MMO MMEH MMRE-EMEMM MEREM MERMPMP MOM MIM MMOW MEH MMIM MMOUT MMOMMEM-MEM!"

says...

*: "...THE TAO (CHINESE="PATH" OR "WAY") THAT **CAN BE NAMED** IS NOT THE **ETERNAL TAO**."

*: "SO WE PRESENT THE FOLLOWING **EXCERPTS** FROM THIS LEGENDARY SAGE'S SPIRITUAL MASTERPIECE, THE **TAO TE CHING** (*"THE BOOK OF THE WAY AND ITS VIRTUE,"* C. 600 B.C.), **WITHOUT** COMMENTARY!"

UNDER HEAVEN ALL CAN SEE BEAUTY **AS** BEAUTY ONLY BECAUSE THERE IS **UGLINESS**.

ALL CAN KNOW GOOD **AS** GOOD ONLY BECAUSE THERE IS **EVIL**.

THEREFORE HAVING AND **NOT** HAVING ARISE **TOGETHER**.

DIFFICULT AND EASY **COMPLIMENT** EACH OTHER.

THEREFORE, THE SAGE GOES ABOUT DOING **NOTHING**, TEACHING **NO-TALKING**.

WORK IS **DONE**, THEN **FORGOTTEN**.

THEREFORE, IT LASTS **FOREVER**.

WHY DO HEAVEN AND EARTH LAST FOREVER?

THEY ARE **UNBORN**, SO EVER **LIVING**.

DO YOU THINK YOU CAN **IMPROVE** THE UNIVERSE?

I DO NOT BELIEVE IT CAN BE DONE.

THE UNIVERSE IS **SACRED**. IF YOU TRY TO CHANGE IT, YOU WILL **RUIN** IT. IF YOU TRY TO **HOLD** IT, YOU WILL **LOSE** IT.

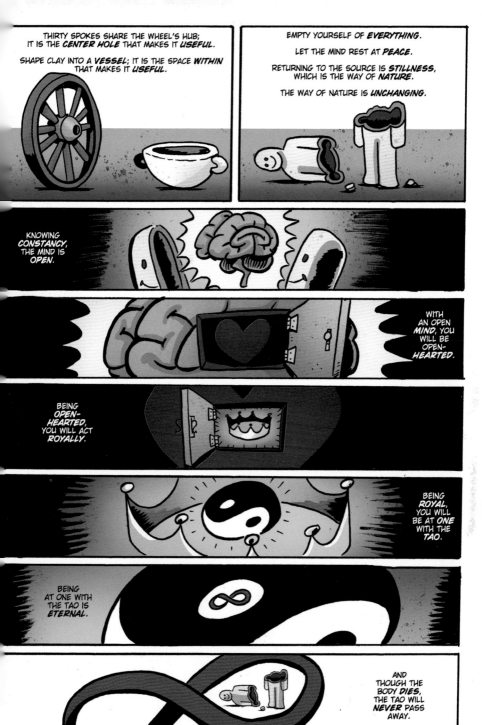

THIRTY SPOKES SHARE THE WHEEL'S HUB; IT IS THE *CENTER HOLE* THAT MAKES IT *USEFUL*.

SHAPE CLAY INTO A *VESSEL*; IT IS THE SPACE *WITHIN* THAT MAKES IT *USEFUL*.

EMPTY YOURSELF OF *EVERYTHING*.

LET THE MIND REST AT *PEACE*.

RETURNING TO THE SOURCE IS *STILLNESS*, WHICH IS THE WAY OF *NATURE*.

THE WAY OF NATURE IS *UNCHANGING*.

KNOWING *CONSTANCY*, THE MIND IS *OPEN*.

WITH AN OPEN *MIND*, YOU WILL BE OPEN-*HEARTED*.

BEING *OPEN-HEARTED*, YOU WILL ACT *ROYALLY*.

BEING *ROYAL*, YOU WILL BE AT *ONE* WITH THE *TAO*.

BEING AT ONE WITH THE TAO IS *ETERNAL*.

AND THOUGH THE BODY *DIES*, THE TAO WILL *NEVER* PASS AWAY.

51

KNOWING **OTHERS**
IS **WISDOM;**

KNOWING THE **SELF**
IS **ENLIGHTENMENT.**

MASTERING OTHERS
REQUIRES **FORCE;**

MASTERING THE SELF
NEEDS **STRENGTH.**

A TRULY **GOOD** MAN
IS NOT **AWARE** OF HIS
GOODNESS, AND IS
THEREFORE GOOD.

A **FOOLISH** MAN
TRIES TO BE GOOD,
AND IS THEREFORE
NOT GOOD.

THOSE WHO **KNOW**
DO NOT **TALK.**

THOSE WHO **TALK**
DO NOT **KNOW.**

KEEP YOUR MOUTH
CLOSED. GUARD YOUR
SENSES. BE AT ONE
WITH THE DUST OF
THE EARTH.

THIS IS
**PRIMAL
UNION.**

A MAN IS **BORN**
GENTLE AND **WEAK.** AT
HIS **DEATH** HE IS HARD
AND **STIFF.**

THEREFORE THE STIFF
AND **UNBENDING** IS THE
DISCIPLE OF **DEATH.**

THE
GENTLE AND
YIELDING IS
THE DISCIPLE
OF **LIFE.**

'COURSE,
MODERN SCHOLARS
NOW BELIEVE THAT NO SUCH
GUY AS "LAO TZU" (WHICH MEANS
"OLD MASTER") EVER REALLY
EXISTED --

HIS **TAO**
IS ACTUALLY
A **COMPILATION**
OF APHORISMS
FROM **MULTIPLE**
AUTHORS!

BUT FOR
AN **APOCRYPHAL** FIGURE
HE SURE IS **CUTE,** AIN'T
HE? COOCHIE-COOCHIE-
COO!

*tee hee
hee!*

52

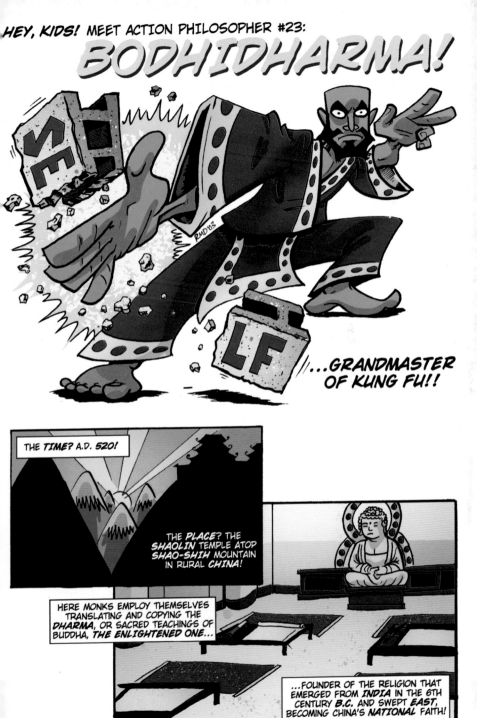

HEY, KIDS! MEET ACTION PHILOSOPHER #23:

BODHIDHARMA!

...GRANDMASTER OF KUNG FU!!

THE *TIME?* A.D. *520!*

THE *PLACE?* THE *SHAOLIN* TEMPLE ATOP *SHAO-SHIH* MOUNTAIN IN RURAL *CHINA!*

HERE MONKS EMPLOY THEMSELVES TRANSLATING AND COPYING THE *DHARMA*, OR SACRED TEACHINGS OF BUDDHA, *THE ENLIGHTENED ONE...*

...FOUNDER OF THE RELIGION THAT EMERGED FROM *INDIA* IN THE 6TH CENTURY *B.C.* AND SWEPT *EAST*, BECOMING CHINA'S *NATIONAL* FAITH!

53

BUT THERE'S NOT A LOT OF **SCRIPTURE-COPYING** GOING ON **TODAY**.

TODAY **SHOULD** BE A **JOYFUL** DAY...

...FOR **BODHIDHARMA** HAS ARRIVED IN CHINA!

THE FAMED PATRIARCH OF THE **DHYANA SCHOOL** OF BUDDHISM DECIDED TO BECOME A POOR MISSIONARY, PREACHING IN FOREIGN LANDS, UPON THE DEATH OF HIS **OWN** TEACHER.

RUMOR HAD IT THAT HE WAS BORN TO VAST **WEALTH** IN CONJEEVERAM, IN SOUTHERN INDIA, BUT HE GAVE IT ALL **UP** TO FOLLOW THE PATH OF THE ENLIGHTENED ONE!

SOME WHISPERED HE WAS SO SINGLE-MINDED THAT HE HAD **WALKED** ALL THE WAY FROM INDIA!

HE WAS GIVEN A GRAND WELCOME BY **EMPEROR WU** HIMSELF! "I HAVE BUILT MANY TEMPLES AND MONASTERIES," THE EMPEROR SAID. "I HAVE COPIED THE **SACRED BOOKS** OF THE BUDDHA. NOW **WHAT** IS MY MERIT?"

AND THIS **UPPITY FOREIGNER** HAD THE TEMERITY TO REPLY:

"NONE **WHATSOEVER,** YOUR MAJESTY!"

SUCH **HERESY** COULD NOT BE ALLOWED INSIDE THE HALLOWED HALLS OF **SHAOLIN TEMPLE!!**

BUT BODHIDHARMA WAS A **PATIENT** MAN.

HE'D WAIT UNTIL THE MONKS **CHANGED THEIR MINDS.**

SLAM!

AND HE WOULD **WAIT...**

AND **WAIT...**

...FOR **NINE LONG YEARS!**

WHOA... HIS GAZE IS SO **INTENSE** IT BORE A **HOLE** IN THE CLIFFSIDE!

MAYBE HE REALLY **DOES** HAVE SOMETHING TO SHOW US!

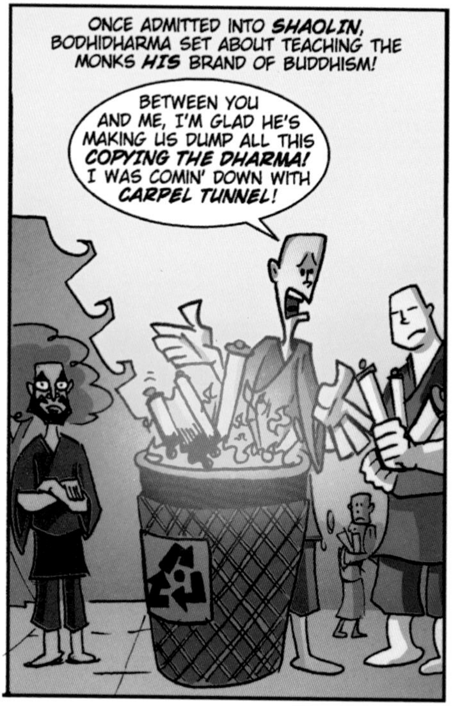
ONCE ADMITTED INTO SHAOLIN, BODHIDHARMA SET ABOUT TEACHING THE MONKS HIS BRAND OF BUDDHISM!
BETWEEN YOU AND ME, I'M GLAD HE'S MAKING US DUMP ALL THIS COPYING THE DHARMA! I WAS COMIN' DOWN WITH CARPEL TUNNEL!

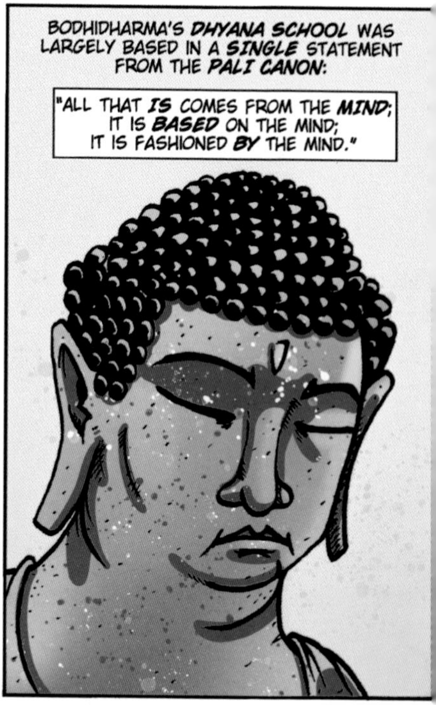
BODHIDHARMA'S DHYANA SCHOOL WAS LARGELY BASED IN A SINGLE STATEMENT FROM THE PALI CANON:
"ALL THAT IS COMES FROM THE MIND; IT IS BASED ON THE MIND; IT IS FASHIONED BY THE MIND."

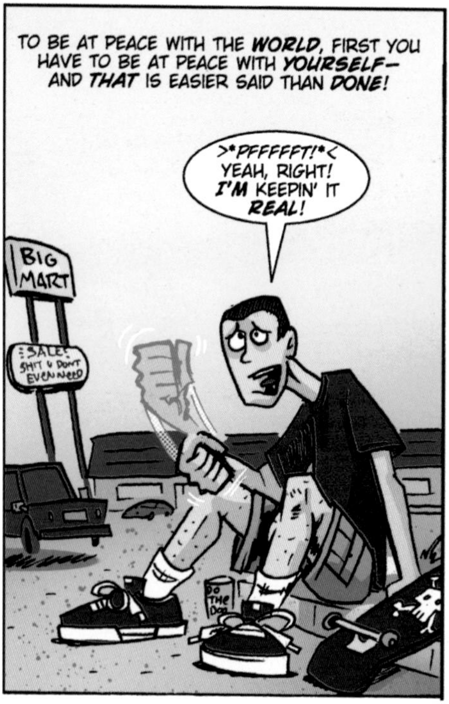
TO BE AT PEACE WITH THE WORLD, FIRST YOU HAVE TO BE AT PEACE WITH YOURSELF– AND THAT IS EASIER SAID THAN DONE!
>*PFFFFFT!*< YEAH, RIGHT! I'M KEEPIN' IT REAL!
BIG MART
SALE! SHIT U DON'T EVEN NEED

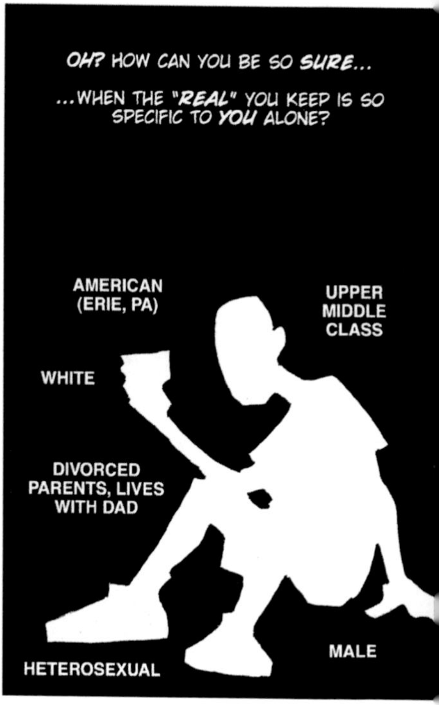
OH? HOW CAN YOU BE SO SURE...
...WHEN THE "REAL" YOU KEEP IS SO SPECIFIC TO YOU ALONE?
AMERICAN (ERIE, PA)
UPPER MIDDLE CLASS
WHITE
DIVORCED PARENTS, LIVES WITH DAD
MALE
HETEROSEXUAL

YOU **PERCEIVE** WHAT IS **REAL** ONLY AS IT IS STRAINED THROUGH YOUR **CONSCIOUSNESS**...

...BUT YOUR CONSCIOUSNESS IS **BIASED** TOWARD YOUR OWN SENSE OF **IDENTITY**, OR **SELF**!

IN **BUDDHISM**, ONLY **ENLIGHTENMENT** - THE ANNIHILATION OF THE **SELF** - CAN **LIBERATE** A PERSON'S CONSCIOUSNESS TO EXPERIENCE UNMEDIATED, **OBJECTIVE** REALITY.

TRADITIONAL BUDDHISM HELD THAT ENLIGHTENMENT WAS A **LIFELONG** PROCESS REQUIRING AN INTENSE **STUDY** OF THE **DHARMA**.

GEEZ, THIS IS TAKING **FOREVER**...

BODHIDHARMA DIDN'T **BUY** THAT. AFTER **ALL**...

THE **BUDDHA** DID NOT HAVE THE DHARMA, YET **HE** BECAME ENLIGHTENED. WHAT DO THE **REST** OF US NEED IT FOR?

57

HIS **DHAYMA** SCHOOL HELD THAT ENLIGHTENMENT COULD ONLY COME IN THE FORM OF AN **INSTANTANEOUS INSIGHT!**

BODHIDHARMA BELIEVED THAT MAINSTREAM BUDDHISTS USED THE BUDDHA'S LESSONS AS A **CRUTCH** THAT ACTUALLY **HINDERED** ENLIGHTENMENT.

HENCE ONE OF HIS MOST FAMOUS **SAYINGS:**

WALK

"IF YOU SEE BUDDHA ON THE ROAD...**KILL HIM!**"

MASTER, PLEASE PACIFY MY **MIND!**

SHOW ME THIS MIND, SO THAT I MAY PACIFY IT.

HUH? BUT I **CAN'T** SHOW YOU MY **MIND!**

WELL, THEN...

THESE RIDDLES, CALLED **"KOANS,"** DEMONSTRATE THE **ABSURDITY** OF TRUTH, AT LEAST INASMUCH AS IT IS UNDERSTOOD BY THE SUBJECTIVE SELF:

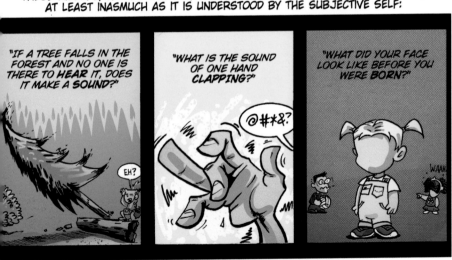

THE POINT ISN'T TO **ANSWER** KOANS, BUT TO CONTEMPLATE WHY THEY **CAN'T** BE ANSWERED!

WORDS AND LANGUAGE ARE ALL COMMUNICATIONS BETWEEN **ONE** SELF TO **ANOTHER**, AND THEREFORE **USELESS**.

IN OTHER WORDS, **"FACTS"** AS WE KNOW THEM ARE **ILLUSIONS**! ALL STATEMENTS ARE **LANGUAGE**, AND BY DEFINITION **OPINIONS**!

POPPYCOCK! THE **SCIENTIFIC METHOD** PROVES THAT WE ARE CAPABLE OF ASCERTAINING **OBJECTIVE** REALITY THROUGH REPEATED **EXPERIMENTATION**!

AH, BUT THE "UNCERTAINLY PRINCIPLE" OF **QUANTUM MECHANICS** PROVES THAT **SUBATOMIC PARTICLES** ALTER THEIR BEHAVIOR WHEN OBSERVED BY RESEARCHERS! EVEN **PHYSICS** IS TAINTED BY THE **SELF**!

REAL TRUTH IS **EXPERIENTIAL**, AND CANNOT BE **MEDIATED**.

IT'S THE ULTIMATE **"YOU HAD TO BE THERE."**

LANGUAGE... SCIENCE... EVEN **ART** IS SUBJECTIVE AND CAN'T BE TRUSTED!

THAT *INCLUDES* THIS COMIC STRIP!!

SORRY.

THE ONLY *TRUTH* CONVEYED BY A LANGUAGE-BASED KOAN IS THE LINGERING *QUESTION MARK* WHERE THE ANSWER WOULD BE... IF ONE *EXISTED!*

CONTEMPLATING THIS IN MEDITATION ALLOWS YOU TO *"ENTER THE SILENCE"*...

...WHEREIN THE *DISTINCTIONS* BETWEEN YOU AND THE REST OF THE WORLD OF WHICH YOU ARE A *PART* BREAK DOWN...

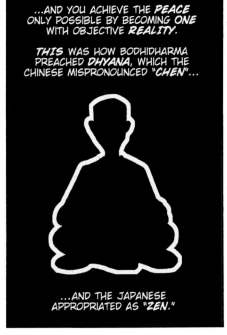

...AND YOU ACHIEVE THE *PEACE* ONLY POSSIBLE BY BECOMING *ONE* WITH OBJECTIVE *REALITY*.

THIS WAS HOW BODHIDHARMA PREACHED *DHYANA*, WHICH THE CHINESE MISPRONOUNCED *"CHEN"*...

...AND THE JAPANESE APPROPRIATED AS *"ZEN."*

LONG-TERM MEDITATION IS AS STRENUOUS *PHYSICALLY* AS IT IS MENTALLY. TO KEEP THE SHAOLIN MONKS IN *PEAK* CONDITION, BODHIDHARMA DEVELOPED STRENUOUS *EXERCISES*.

HIS CHARGES RIGHTLY CALLED THESE "HARD WORK..."

...OR, IN CHINESE, *"KUNG FU!"*

NOBODY KNOWS IF BODHIDHARMA ACTUALLY *INTENDED* FOR HIS EXERCISES TO BE DEVELOPED INTO A *PERSONAL DEFENSE SYSTEM*...

...BUT THE LEGENDARY ABILITY OF THE MARTIAL ARTS MASTER TO SIMPLY *REACT* AND *DEFLECT* BLOWS AS THEY'RE AIMED AT HIM IS A *PERFECT* EXAMPLE OF THE ZEN IDEAL OF *ANNIHILATING* THE DISTINCTIONS BETWEEN YOURSELF AND THE REST OF THE WORLD!

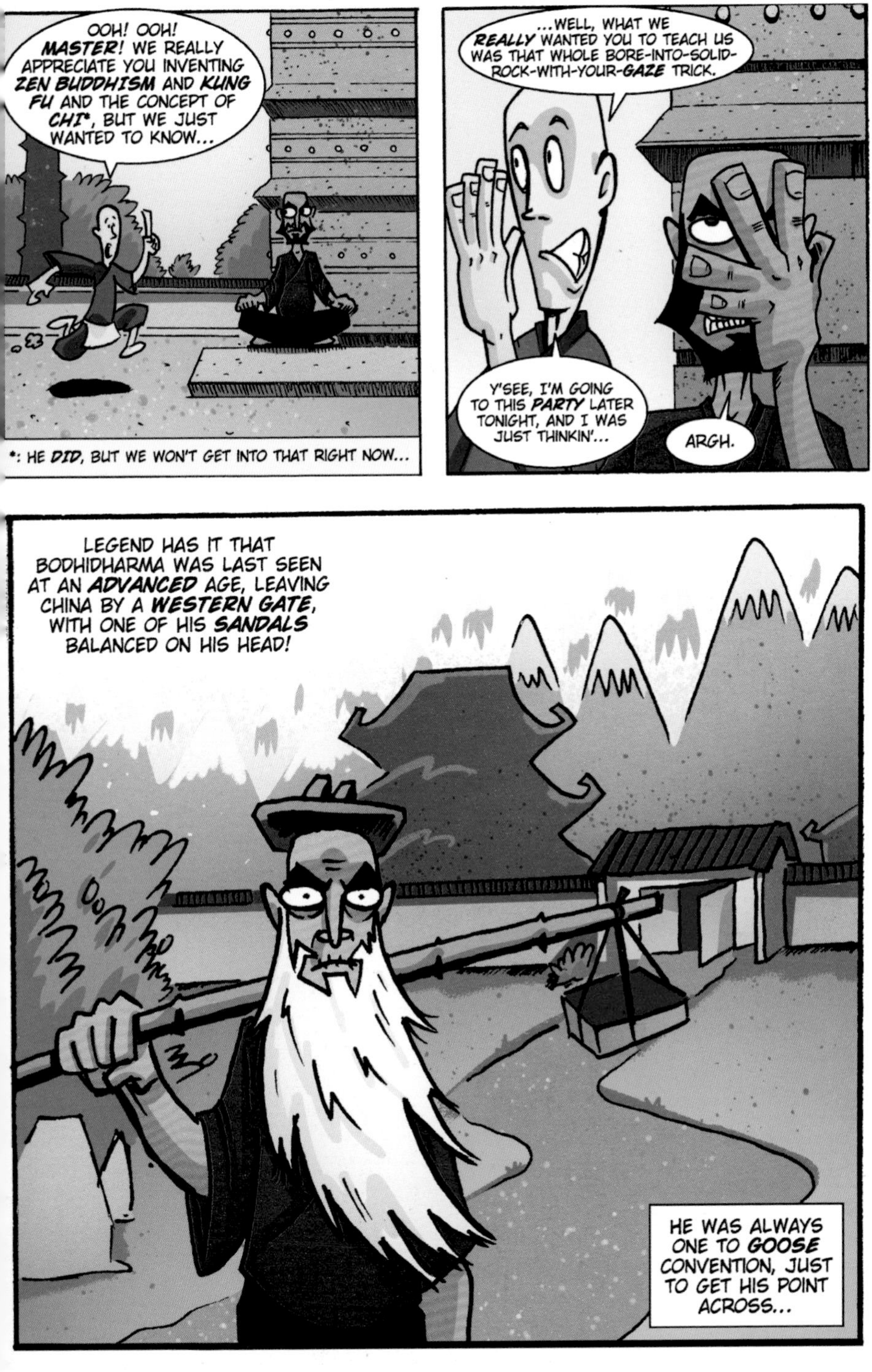

OOH! OOH! MASTER! WE REALLY APPRECIATE YOU INVENTING ZEN BUDDHISM AND KUNG FU AND THE CONCEPT OF CHI*, BUT WE JUST WANTED TO KNOW...
*: HE DID, BUT WE WON'T GET INTO THAT RIGHT NOW...
...WELL, WHAT WE REALLY WANTED YOU TO TEACH US WAS THAT WHOLE BORE-INTO-SOLID-ROCK-WITH-YOUR-GAZE TRICK.
Y'SEE, I'M GOING TO THIS PARTY LATER TONIGHT, AND I WAS JUST THINKIN'...
ARGH.
LEGEND HAS IT THAT BODHIDHARMA WAS LAST SEEN AT AN ADVANCED AGE, LEAVING CHINA BY A WESTERN GATE, WITH ONE OF HIS SANDALS BALANCED ON HIS HEAD!
HE WAS ALWAYS ONE TO GOOSE CONVENTION, JUST TO GET HIS POINT ACROSS...

LOOK CLOSELY AT *JALAL UD-DIN MUHAMMAD RUMI!* AT THE MOMENT HE IS MERELY A 37 YEAR-OLD PREACHER AND TEACHER OF THEOLOGY AT A LOCAL *MADRASSA,* AN ISLAMIC RELIGIOUS SCHOOL, IN KONYA, TURKEY!

BUT YOU ARE NOW WITNESS TO THE FINAL MOMENT OF THIS PHASE OF HIS EXISTENCE! FOR THE DATE IS *NOVEMBER 15, 1244!* WITHIN MOMENTS HE WILL BE TRANSFORMED INTO *ACTION PHILOSOPHER #26,* KNOWN IN THE WEST SIMPLY AS...

RUMI!

SUDDENLY, A FIGURE LUNGED AT HIM FROM A DOORWAY, STARTLING HIM WITH THE QUESTION:

WHO IS **GREATER,** MUHAMMAD OR BESTAMI?

THE COMPARISON WAS BETWEEN THE LEGENDARY PROPHET WHO FOUNDED ISLAM (570-632) AND FAMED 9TH CENTURY MYSTIC *BAYAZID AL-BESTAMI* (D. 874).

BESTAMI WAS AN ADHERENT OF *SUFISM,* THE MUSLIM MYSTIC TRADITION WHICH TEACHES ONE CAN DRAW CLOSER TO GOD IN THIS LIFE BY STRIVING TO ACHIEVE WHAT THE QUR'AN CALLS *FITRA--*

--A *"PURE STATE"* OF ORIGINAL HUMAN NATURE IN WHICH ALL OF ONE'S ACTIONS ARE MOTIVATED SOLELY BY A *LOVE FOR GOD* -- DESTROYING ONE'S SELF IN ORDER TO UNIFY ONE'S WILL *WITH* THE DIVINE.

WHEN ASKED HOW OLD HE WAS, BESTAMI WOULD REPLY *"FOUR"*, BECAUSE:

"I HAVE BEEN VEILED FROM GOD BY THIS WORLD FOR *SEVENTY* YEARS, BUT I HAVE SEEN HIM DURING THE LAST *FOUR* YEARS;

"THE PERIOD IN WHICH ONE IS *VEILED* DOES NOT BELONG TO ONE'S LIFE!"

IN FACT, BESTAMI WENT SO FAR AS TO CLAIM THAT IN HIS ECSTATIC STATE HE BECAME *ONE* WITH GOD, CRYING OUT:

I AM THE GLORY!

NEVERTHELESS, IT BORDERED ON BLASPHEMY TO PLACE ONE ABOVE MUHAMMAD, "THE ANOINTED ONE," SO WHEN CHALLENGED, RUMI REPLIED IN THE EXPECTED MANNER:

MUHAMMAD, OF COURSE!

BUT BESTAMI SAID, *"I AM THE GLORY!"* MUHAMMAD SAID, *"I CANNOT PRAISE YOU ENOUGH!"*

THE DISTINCTION WAS THAT A PROPHET, NO MATTER HOW GREAT, IS STILL A *MESSENGER* -- AS OPPOSED TO ONE WHO RECEIVES THE MESSAGE *INSTANTLY*, WITHOUT MEDIATION!

AT SOON AS RUMI RECEIVED *THIS* MESSAGE HE FELL SENSELESS FROM HIS HORSE!

QED!

LATER, HE WOULD SAY, "WHAT I ONCE THOUGHT OF AS *GOD* I MET TODAY AS A *HUMAN BEING!*"

BESTAMI TOOK *ONE* SWALLOW OF KNOWLEDGE AND THOUGHT THAT WAS ALL...

...BUT FOR *MUHAMMAD* THE MAJESTY WAS CONTINUALLY *UNFOLDING!*

YES, YES...*YOU* ARE THE ONE I AM LOOKING FOR!

THE ENIGMATIC *DERVISH*, OR WANDERING SUFI HOLY MAN, WAS *SHAMS-E TABRIZI* ("SHAMS" = "SUN" IN ARABIC).

SHAMS' RELIGIOUS **BLUNTNESS** DID NOT ENDEAR HIM TO THOSE HE MET ON HIS TRAVELS.

HIS NICKNAME WAS *"THE BIRD"* BECAUSE HE NEVER STAYED IN ONE PLACE FOR TOO LONG.

LEGEND HAS IT HE FINALLY PRAYED IN **DESPAIR:**

WHERE O WHERE MAY I FIND ONE WHO CAN **ENDURE** MY COMPANY?

WHAT WILL YOU GIVE IN **RETURN?**

WHY, MY VERY **HEAD!**

THEN THE ONE YOU SEEK IS JALAL UD-DIN OF KONYA!

GREAT!

YOU GOT A **STREET ADDRESS,** OR...?

SHAMS BECAME RUMI'S TEACHER AND RUMI BECAME THE INSEPARABLE FRIEND SHAMS HAD LONG SOUGHT. THEY SPENT MONTHS-LONG RETREATS IN SOLITUDE TOGETHER, MEDITATING AND DISCUSSING THEOLOGY.

THEY'RE SO TOTALLY TALKING ABOUT **US** IN THERE, I JUST KNOW IT!

RUMI'S OWN STUDENTS BECAME INTENSELY JEALOUS, CONVINCING THEMSELVES THEIR TEACHER HAD FALLEN UNDER THE SPELL OF A MADMAN AND A CHARLATAN.

FINALLY, ON THE NIGHT OF DECEMBER 5, 1248...

HEY! THEY'RE HANDING **FREE RUGS** OUT HERE!

RUGS? **WHERE?!**

...SHAMS **VANISHED** THROUGH THE BACK DOOR OF THE HOME HE SHARED WITH RUMI, NEVER TO BE SEEN AGAIN.

DUDE! NO FAIR!

AND THUS THE PROPHECY WAS FULFILLED.

66

RUMI WAS INCONSOLABLE OVER HIS FRIEND'S DISAPPEARANCE.

SHAAAAAMS? WHERE AAAAAAARE YOU?

HE TRAVELED ACROSS THE MIDDLE EAST LOOKING FOR HIM, UNTIL, IN DAMASCUS, HE REACHED HIS *SECOND GREAT REALIZATION:*

I *NEVER* LOST SHAMS AT ALL! HE'S *INSIDE* ME THROUGH HIS TEACHINGS!

UH... COULD YOU LET ME OUT, THEN? IT'S *STUFFY* IN HERE...

FROM RUMI'S PEN BEGAN TO FLOW *POETRY* THAT IMMORTALIZED THEIR FRIENDSHIP... AND EXPLICATED THEIR RELIGIOUS TEACHINGS!

RUMI'S VERSE URGES US TO GET BEYOND OUR OWN SELFISH HUMAN *EGOS* TO THE TIME *BEFORE* THE FALL FROM PARADISE, WHEN MAN'S MIND AND *GOD'S* MIND WERE ONE!

I'M THINKING OF A NUMBER BETWEEN ONE AND *ONE BILLION*--

585,463,930?

DUUUUDE! WE ARE SO, LIKE, IN *SYNC!*

TO EVOKE THE INTENSELY *PERSONAL* AND *PASSIONATE* NATURE OF RELIGIOUS EXPERIENCE, RUMI PROCLAIMS THIS CONDUIT BETWEEN SELFISH ISOLATION AND DIVINE UNITY TO BE *LOVE!*

"I AM IN LOVE WITH LOVE AND LOVE IS IN LOVE WITH ME..."

Date-A -GOD.NET

VITALS

TURN-ONS
-WRATH
-FLOODS
-THY NEIGHBOR

TURN-OFFS
-GRAVEN IMAGES
-FALSE IDOLS
-FAT CHICKS

AND THE ECSTATIC EGO-LESS STATE OF RELIGIOUS RAPTURE RUMI REFERS TO AS *"DRUNKENNESS"--* A *DARING* METAPHOR IN ISLAM!

CHUG! CHUG! CHUG!

"I DRANK THAT WINE OF WHICH THE SOUL IS ITS *VESSEL*," HE WRITES. "ITS *ECSTASY* HAS STOLEN MY *INTELLECT* AWAY."

AND FOR RUMI, THE *NARRATOR* OF THE POEMS, IT IS HIS LOVE FOR SHAMS -- *"THE SUN"* -- THAT SHINES THROUGH!

"WHO SAYS THAT THE *IMMORTAL ONE* HAS DIED? / WHO SAYS THAT THE *SUN OF HOPE* HAS DIED?

"LOOK, IT IS THE *ENEMY* OF THE SUN WHO HAS COME TO THE ROOFTOP! / CLOSING BOTH EYES SHUT, CRYING:

"O, THE SUN HAS DIED!!"

RUMI'S VERSE IS AS PASSIONATE AND SENSUAL AS ANY *POP SONG.*

"OH GOD-- LET ALL LOVERS BE CONTENT--GIVE THEM HAPPY ENDINGS--LET THEIR LIVES BE CELEBRATIONS!

"LET THEIR HEARTS DANCE IN THE FIRE OF YOUR LOVE!"

IT IS ALSO INTENSELY *MYSTICAL:*

"UNTIL A DISCIPLE *ANNIHILATES* HIMSELF COMPLETELY, UNION WILL NOT BE *REVEALED* TO HIM.

UNION CANNOT BE *PENETRATED.*

IT IS YOUR OWN *DESTRUCTION.*

OTHERWISE, EVERY *WORTHLESS* PERSON WOULD BECOME THE *TRUTH."*

68

THOUGH PROUDLY **MUSLIM**, RUMI'S POETRY SPEAKS THE LANGUAGE OF GOD AND LOVE SO **PLAINLY** IT HAS BEEN EMBRACED BY PEOPLE OF EVERY FAITH ALL AROUND THE WORLD!

"TODAY IS BRIGHT AND ILLUMINATING, ILLUMINATING, ILLUMINATING!"

"THIS LOVE IS UNIFYING, UNIFYING, UNIFYING!"

"AND IT'S BIDDING THE INTELLECT FAREWELL, FAREWELL, FAREWELL!"

"TODAY IT'S TIME FOR SAMAA, FOR SAMAA, FOR SAMAA!

"SAMAA" REFERS TO THE SPINNING DANCE OF THE MOST **FAMOUS** OF RUMI'S FOLLOWERS, THE **WHIRLING DERVISHES!**

"THE LOVER LIKE THE **ATOMS** WILL TURN..."

THEIR SPINNING SYMBOLIZES NOT JUST RELIGIOUS ECSTASY-- A FORM OF **DKHIR**, OR REMEMBRANCE OF GOD...

-- BUT **UNITY** WITH THE **UNIVERSE!** AFTER ALL, THE PLANETS -- THE STARS -- OUR **GALAXY** ITSELF IS IN A CONSTANT STATE OF **REVOLUTION!**

"...WHEN THE SPRING BREEZE OF **LOVE** BEGINS TO SWIRL..."

THE DERVISHES, OR THE **MEVLEVI ORDER**, WERE FOUNDED BY RUMI'S FOLLOWERS NOT LONG AFTER HIS DEATH IN 1273.

HE LEFT BEHIND TWO VOLUMINOUS WORKS OF POETRY, **SPIRITUAL COUPLETS** AND **THE COMPLETE WORKS OF SHAMS OF TABRIZ.**

FOR THE LAST TEN YEARS OR MORE, RUMI HAS BEEN THE MOST **POPULAR** POET IN THE UNITED STATES, SELLING WELL OVER A **HALF A MILLION COPIES!**

"...ANY BRANCH THAT IS **NOT DEAD** WILL **DANCE!**"

RUMI
RUMI
RUMI
RUMI

OY, VEY! ACTION PHILOSOPHER #12 IS **ISAAC LURIA,** A/K/A YITZHAK BEN SOLOMON ASHKENAZI, A/K/A **ARI,** A/K/A:

RABBI OF THE MYSTIC ARTS!

THOUGH BORN IN **JERUSALEM** IN 1534, ISAAC SPENT HIS CHILDHOOD IN **EGYPT,** WHERE HE GREW INTO A HIGHLY **DEVOUT** YOUNG MAN!

HE SPENT **SEVEN YEARS** STUDYING ANCIENT TOMES OF JUDAIC WISDOM ON THE BANKS OF THE **NILE** ... INCLUDING THE FAMOUS **ZOHAR!**

THIS "BOOK OF RADIANCE" FIRST APPEARED IN **SPAIN** IN THE 1200'S, PUBLISHED BY ONE **MOSES DE LEON.**

A 1,000-YEAR-OLD COLLECTION OF MEDITATIONS ON THE TORAH, DISCOVERED BY **ME!** VERY **RARE!** A **STEAL** AT FIFTY PESETAS!

ZOHAR

(AFTER DE LEON **DIED,** THOUGH, HIS WIFE CONFESSED **HE** WAS THE TRUE AUTHOR!)

LIKE THE PLACEBO THAT ACTUALLY *CURES* THE PATIENT, HOWEVER, DE LEON'S *ZOHAR* SPARKED THE SCHOOL OF JEWISH MYSTICAL THOUGHT KNOWN AS *THE KABBALAH*, WHICH MEANS...

TRADITIOOOOON! TRADITION!

...OR, MORE LITERALLY, *"THAT WHICH IS RECEIVED."*

KABBALISTS, FOLLOWING THE *ZOHAR*, REFER TO THE JEWISH GOD AS *EIN SOF*--

I *THINK* GOD'S DOWN THERE *SOMEWHERE...* ~GULP!~

--AN ESSENTIALLY UNKNOWABLE *"INFINITE"* FROM WHICH ALL CREATION *EMANATES*.

CONTEMPLATING EIN SOF ALONG THE NILE, ISAAC HAD A VISION OF THE PROPHET *ELIJAH*...

THE TIME FOR STUDYING IS *OVER!* YOU MUST NOW GO *OUT* INTO THE WORLD, AND SHARE WHAT YOU'VE LEARNED WITH GOD'S *CHOSEN PEOPLE!*

BUT FIRST... TAKE A *SHOWER*, WILLYA? PEE-YEW!

THE LURIAS DECAMPED FOR *ISRAEL*, SPECIFICALLY *SAFED*, A SMALL TOWN IN THE MOUNTAINS OF GAILILEE AND A *HOTBED* OF KABBALIST STUDY.

ISAAC'S STUDENTS CALLED HIM *ARI*-- A HEBREW ACRONYM FOR "OUR MASTER RABBI ISAAC" THAT ALSO MEANS *"LION"*--

-- SO THEY CALLED THEMSELVES THE *"CUBS!"*

THIS *TREE OF LIFE* IS THE COSMIC *FLOWCHART* BY WHICH EIN SOF *EMANATES* REALITY--

--I CALL EACH *STAGE* OF THAT PROCESS A *SEFIRAH*, OR *"ENUMERATION!"*

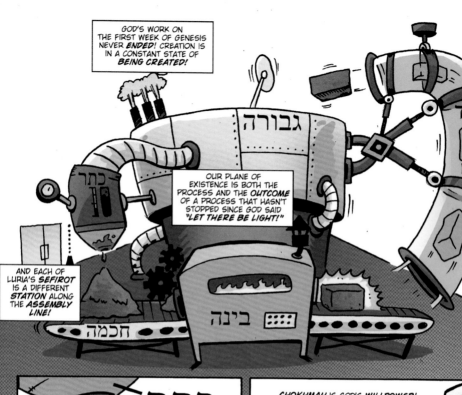

GOD'S WORK ON THE FIRST WEEK OF GENESIS NEVER **ENDED!** CREATION IS IN A CONSTANT STATE OF **BEING CREATED!**

OUR PLANE OF EXISTENCE IS BOTH THE PROCESS AND THE **OUTCOME** OF A PROCESS THAT HASN'T STOPPED SINCE GOD SAID **"LET THERE BE LIGHT!"**

AND EACH OF LURIA'S **SEFIROT** IS A DIFFERENT **STATION** ALONG THE **ASSEMBLY LINE!**

KETER, "THE CROWN", IS THE SEFIRAH AT WHICH CREATION FIRST RECEIVES THE SPARK OF **POSSIBILITY.**

KETER IS PURE **CREATIVITY** -- AT THIS POINT, **ANYTHING** CAN HAPPEN!

CHOKHMAH IS GOD'S **WILLPOWER!** IT GIVES GOD'S THOUGHTS THE ABILITY TO **ACTUALIZE** THEIR POTENTIAL.

FROM CHOKHMAH, THEY PASS ON TO **BINAH**, THE MOTHER OF FORM, WHICH GRANTS GOD'S THOUGHTS THE **POTENTIALITY** OF PHYSICAL MANIFESTATION.

THE **INSPIRATION** OF GOD, **CHESED**, CHANNELS GOD'S IDEAS TOWARD A **SPECIFIC** FORM.

גבורה

BEFORE ANYTHING *NEW* CAN BE CREATED, THE *OLD* MUST BE DONE AWAY WITH.

GEVURAH IS THE GREAT *DESTROYER* OF THE SEFIROT...

... WHILE *TIPHERETH* IS THE GREAT *BALANCER* ... THE *RATIONAL* PART OF THE DIVINE MIND!

תפארת

BY PASSING THROUGH *NETZACH* GOD'S IDEAS PICK UP THE QUALITY OF *DESIRE* -- THE URGE TO *CREATE* -- THAT *MOTIVATES* CREATION!

נצח

IF NETZACH *GRANTS* URGES, *HOD* ARTICULATES THEM!

הוד

HOD IS THE *ANALYTICAL* PART OF GOD'S MIND, GIVING FORM TO HIS IDEAS IN THE REALM OF LANGUAGE, LOGIC AND THE *ABSTRACT*.

YESOD SPECIFIES THE PLATONIC FORMS THAT GOD'S IDEAS MAY TAKE; BUT THEY ARE SPECIFIC-*GENERIC*, AS OPPOSED TO SPECIFIC-*INDIVIDUAL*.

יסוד

NOW 100% MOR REAL!!!

REALITY

ALSO KNOWN AS "THE KINGDOM", *MALKUTH* IS THE "OUTPUT TRAY" OF THE TREE OF LIFE, THE *FINAL* MANIFESTATION OF GOD'S THOUGHTS INTO *CORPOREAL REALITY*.

"THE WORD MADE FLESH," AS THE BIBLE SAYS, AND MALKUTH ENCOMPASSES THE FLESH OF THE *ENTIRE PHYSICAL UNIVERSE*!

מלכות

NO DOUBT YOU'VE NOTICED THAT THE SEFIROT ARE ALL NAMED FOR *HEBREW CHARACTERS.*

OY!

KABBALISTS BELIEVE THAT THE HEBREW LANGUAGE--THE LANGUAGE OF THE *TORAH*--IS AS *DIVINELY INSPIRED* AS THE SCRIPTURES *THEMSELVES!*

HEBREW LITERALLY *GIVES LIFE* IN THE OLD FOLKTALE OF *THE GOLEM.*

A KABBALIST RABBI ANIMATES A CLAY STATUE BY WRITING THE HEBREW WORD FOR *"TRUTH"* ON ITS FOREHEAD!

WHEN THE GOLEM'S WORK IS DONE, THE RABBI TURNS HIS CREATION BACK INTO INANIMATE CLAY BY ERASING THE *FIRST LETTER,* THUS SPELLING *METH,* OR *"DEATH!"*

(IN THE *BROTHERS GRIMM* VERSION OF THE TALE, THE GOLEM GROWS *TOO TALL* FOR THE RABBI TO REACH HIS FOREHEAD ...LEADING TO *DISASTROUS RESULTS!)*

THE HEBREW TEXT OF THE TORAH IS THE *ASSEMBLY LANGUAGE* FOR REALITY! SOME KABBALISTS HOLD THAT IF ALL ITS LETTERS WERE TO BE *REARRANGED,* THE SECRETS OF THE UNIVERSE WOULD BE *UNLOCKED*... THE MOST *SIGNIFICANT* BEING THE *TRUE NAME OF GOD.* IT IS CONSIDERED *BLASPHEMOUS* TO SPEAK THIS NAME ALOUD, SO IT IS REPRESENTED IN MOST BIBLES AS JUST *FOUR CONSONANTS*...

... THE SO-CALLED *"TETRAGRAMMATON"* IN HEBREW, *"YHWH"* LOOKS LIKE THE THIRD PERSON SINGULAR IMPERFECT OF THE VERB "TO BE" ... SO THE JEWISH GO[D] IS A *LIVING GOD,* ALWAYS IN THE PROCESS OF *BECOMING!*

THIS IS BECAUSE THE TREE OF LIFE IS A *TWO-WAY* CONDUIT TO THE INFINITE.

JUST AS WHAT GOD DOES AFFECTS *US*, WHAT *WE* DO AFFECTS *HIM*, AND, BY EXTENSION, *REALITY!*

BY CLEAVING *TOWARDS* GOD, DOING *GOOD WORKS*, AND LEADING A PIOUS LIFE, A HUMAN BEING *HELPS* GOD, AND THEREFORE CREATION, INTO A MORE FULLY *REALIZED* STATE.

SNIFF, SNIFF! WE'RE *GETTING* THERE...

CONVERSELY, EVIL, *SELFISH* ACTIONS IMPEDE THE FLOW OF CREATION, AND ARE *DETRIMENTAL* TO GOD.

>ERRK!< I'M GETTIN' *VERKLEMPT* HERE! STAY OUTTA YOUR MOTHER'S PURSE, SHLOMO!

OY!

LURIA HIMSELF WAS SAID TO POSSESS MANY *MYSTICAL POWERS* DERIVING FROM HIS ABILITY TO INFLUENCE THE *FLOW* OF REALITY.

"THE ELEMENTS OF *TIME, SPACE*, AND *MOTION* ARE MERELY AN EXPRESSION OF THE *LIMITATIONS* IMPOSED BY THE PHYSICAL BODY ON THE *SOUL*."

"WHEN THE *SOUL* HAS SWAY OVER THE *BODY*, THESE LIMITING FACTORS *CEASE TO EXIST*."

"LET US NOW PROCEED TO *JERUSALEM*, FOR OUR *PHYSICAL BODIES* HAVE LOST THEIR INFLUENCE OVER OUR *SOULS!*"

BEAM ME UP, ISAAC!

LURIA DIED IN 1572 AT THE AGE OF 38 WITHOUT HAVING WRITTEN ANYTHING *DOWN*.

WAIT! DON'T KICK OFF JUST *YET*--LET ME GET DOWN THAT LAST BIT OF *WISDOM*--

GAK!

DAMMIT!

BUT THE CUBS CAPTURED AS MANY OF HIS TEACHINGS AS THEY COULD IN THE SIX VOLUMES OF *THE TREE OF LIFE*, WHICH SOON SPREAD THROUGHOUT THE *JEWISH WORLD*.

WHILE THE OTHER MONOTHEISTIC RELIGIONS HAVE HAD A TENDENCY TO NEGLECT OR *PERSECUTE* THEIR OWN MYSTICAL TRADITIONS, MAINSTREAM JUDIASM HAS ALWAYS AT LEAST *TOLERATED* THE KABBALAH.

SUFISM

GNOSTICISM

NOT THAT THERE HAVEN'T BEEN A FEW *BUMPS IN THE ROAD*.

YHWH!

A LURIANIC KABBALIST NAMED *SABBATAI ZEVI* CAUSED A MAJOR SCHISM BETWEEN RABBINICAL JUDIASM AND THE JEWISH MASSES IN THE 1600'S BY PROCLAIMING HIMSELF THE *MESSIAH*.

EVEN AFTER ZEVI CONVERTED TO *ISLAM* (OUCH), THE *REBELLIOUS SPIRIT* HE ENGENDERED *PERSISTED*, CULMINATING IN THE FOUNDATION OF THE *HASIDIC* MOVEMENT AROUND 1740...

...USING LITURGY DEVELOPED BY *LURIA* TO CREATE A LESS *SCHOLARSHIP-BOUND* JUDIASM THAT (THEY FELT) CONNECTED BETTER TO THE MASSES' *SPIRITUAL NEEDS*!

PRAISE BE TO *ALLAH*!

FEH! WHO *NEEDS* 'IM?

THE *TREE OF LIFE* INFLUENCED *CHRISTIAN* THOUGHT AS WELL...PARTICULARLY AMONG *ALCHEMISTS* WHO WERE TRYING TO INFLUENCE CREATION IN RATHER *MATERIAL* WAYS...

NOPE. STILL *LEAD.*

YOU KNOW, WE REALLY SUCK AT THIS.

AND, OF COURSE, THE RECENT FASCINATION OF MANY *CELEBRITIES* WITH THE KABBALAH, SPEARHEADED BY *MADONNA,* HAS BEEN WELL-PUBLICIZED.

TABLOIDS REPORTED THAT POP STAR *BRITNEY SPEARS* PLANNED TO GIVE BIRTH TO HER FIRST CHILD IN A POOL FILLED WITH *ONE THOUSAND* ONE-LITER BOTTLES OF SPECIALLY BLESSED *"KABBALAH WATER!"* (AT A PRICE TAG OF *$3,800!*)

ROSEANNE, NAOMI CAMPBELL, ELIZABETH TAYLOR AND BARBARA STREISAND HAVE *ALL* MADE TRIPS TO THE IMMENSELY *TRENDY* KABBALAH CENTRE IN L.A.

RABBI LURIA WAS ONLY WITH US FOR A *SHORT TIME,* SO IT'S HARD TO SAY WHAT HE'D *MAKE* OF ALL THIS SUDDEN ATTENTION. OUR *BEST GUESS* IS...

REMEMBER, BUBELAH, JUST BECAUSE FAMOUS PEOPLE LIKE IT...

...DON'T MEAN IT AIN'T TRUE!

MAZEL TOV!

THOUGH KNOWN IN THE WEST AS *CONFUCIUS* (551-479 B.C.), THIS LEGENDARY CHINESE THINKER IS BETTER KNOWN IN HIS NATIVE LAND AS *KONGZI* WHICH LITERALLY TRANSLATES TO...

MASTER KONG

WHAT LITTLE IS KNOWN OF CONFUCIUS'S LIFE SUGGESTS HE SERVED AS A *SHI*, OR MIDDLE-CLASS *RETAINER*, DURING CHINA'S "DAYS OF SPRING AND AUTUMN" (800-400 B.C.) ...

...WHEN PETTY *TRIBAL KINGS* WARRED OVER THE FRAGMENTS OF THE COLLAPSED *ZHOU* DYNASTY.

THESE *FEUDAL THUGS* WERE EAGER TO ADD LEGITIMACY AND RESPECTABILITY TO THEIR REIGNS BY LEARNING THE COURT ETIQUETTE AND DIPLOMATIC PROTOCOL OF THE *ZHOUS* FROM ITERANT SCHOLARS LIKE CONFUCIUS.

CONFUCIUS'S TEACHINGS WERE COLLECTED IN THE *"FIVE CLASSICS"*, WHICH ULTIMATELY BECAME THE NATIONAL STANDARD OF TRADITIONAL *CHINESE ETHICS.*

AS EARLY AS 136 B.C., THE FIVE CLASSICS WERE *MANDATORY* READING FOR *ALL* WOULD-BE CIVIL SERVANTS.

78

CENTRAL TO CONFUCIAN THOUGHT IS THE IDEA THAT THE MANDATE OF *TIAN* ("HEAVEN") IS THE SAME AS MORAL GOOD...

...BUT ONLY THROUGH *HUMAN AGENCY* MAY THAT MANDATE BE ACTUALIZED HERE ON EARTH!

THUS, CONFUCIANISM IS FUNDAMENTALLY *DIDACTIC,* REINFORCING AESTHETIC, MORAL AND SOCIAL *ORDER* VIA *LI,* OR RITUAL PROPRIETY.

GOOD *MANNERS,* FOR INSTANCE, SATISFY ALL THREE FORMS OF ORDER: THEY *LOOK* GOOD (AESTHETIC), AND THEY MAKE YOU *FEEL* GOOD (MORAL) BECAUSE THEY MAKE *OTHERS* FEEL GOOD (SOCIAL).

KEEPING IN MIND THIS IDEA OF *CONTINUITY* OF *ORDER,* THEN, IT SHOULD COME AS NO SURPRISE TO LEARN THAT CONFUCIUS UPHELD *OBEDIENCE* TO ONE'S *ELDERS* (*XIAO,* OR "FILIAL PIETY") AS THE *HIGHEST* VIRTUE.

IN THE FIRST BOOK OF HIS *ANALECTS* CONFUCIUS WRITES, "OBSERVE WHAT A PERSON HAS IN MIND TO DO WHEN HIS FATHER IS *ALIVE,* AND THEN OBSERVE WHAT HE DOES WHEN HIS FATHER IS *DEAD.*"

"IF, FOR *THREE YEARS,* HE MAKES *NO* CHANGES TO HIS FATHER'S WAYS, HE CAN BE SAID TO BE A *GOOD SON.*"

THERE'S A *TRICKLE-DOWN* EFFECT TO ALL THIS FILIAL PIETY: A *GOOD SON* WILL BE A *GOOD FATHER* AND LIKEWISE RAISE A *GOOD SON*.

A GOOD *MONARCH* WILL ALLOW HIS *GOODNESS* TO FLOW OUT TO HIS *SUBJECTS*.

THUS *MORAL FORCE* (DE) IS *CONTAGIOUS*.

THE *"PROFOUND MAN"* (JUNZI) EXERTS *DE*, THEREFORE MANIFESTS *VIRTUE* (JEN), THEREFORE FULFILLS *TIAN*:

"THE PROFOUND MAN ... DOES NOT SET HIS MIND EITHER *FOR* ANYTHING, OR *AGAINST* ANYTHING; WHAT IS *RIGHT* HE WILL FOLLOW," WRITES CONFUCIUS.

BUT THE *XIAOREN*, THE *SMALL MAN*, HE'S NOT WITH THE PROGRAM:

"THE PROFOUND MAN UNDERSTANDS WHAT IS *MORAL*; THE SMALL MAN UNDERSTANDS WHAT IS *PROFITABLE*." (ANALECTS 4:16)

"WHAT THE PROFOUND MAN SEEKS IS IN *HIMSELF*. WHAT THE SMALL MAN SEEKS IS IN *OTHERS*." (15:20)

SO WHAT'S THE *MORAL* OF MASTER KONG'S STORY? THAT'S RIGHT:

THE SMALL MAN *SUCKS*.

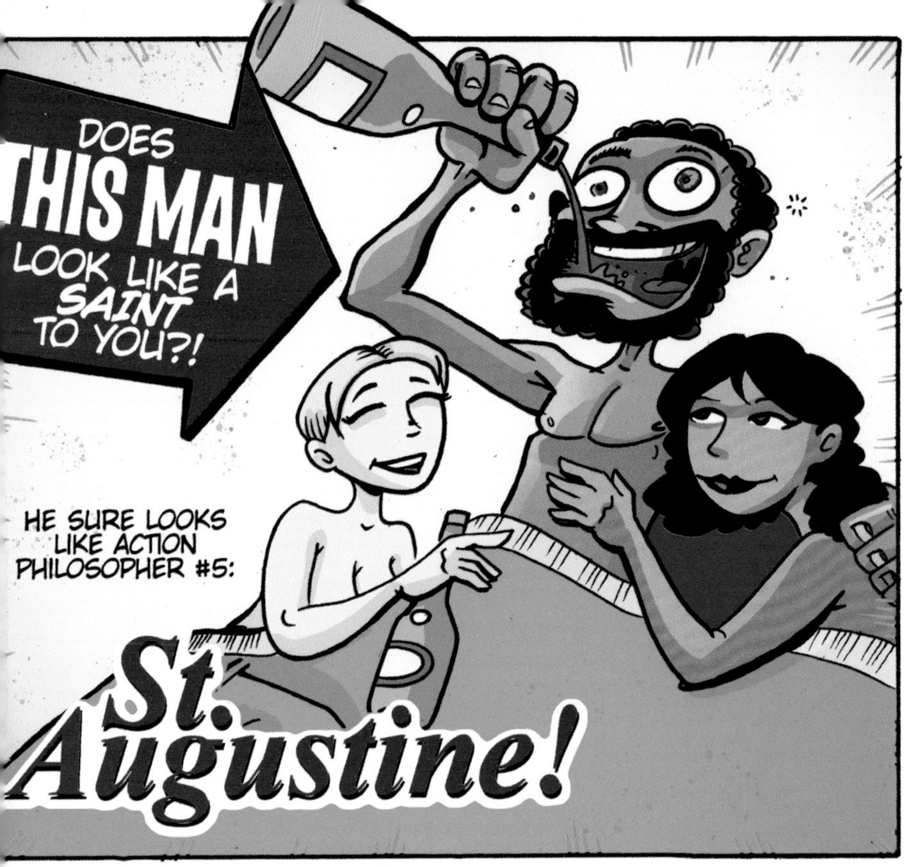
DOES THIS MAN LOOK LIKE A SAINT TO YOU?!
HE SURE LOOKS LIKE ACTION PHILOSOPHER #5:
St. Augustine!

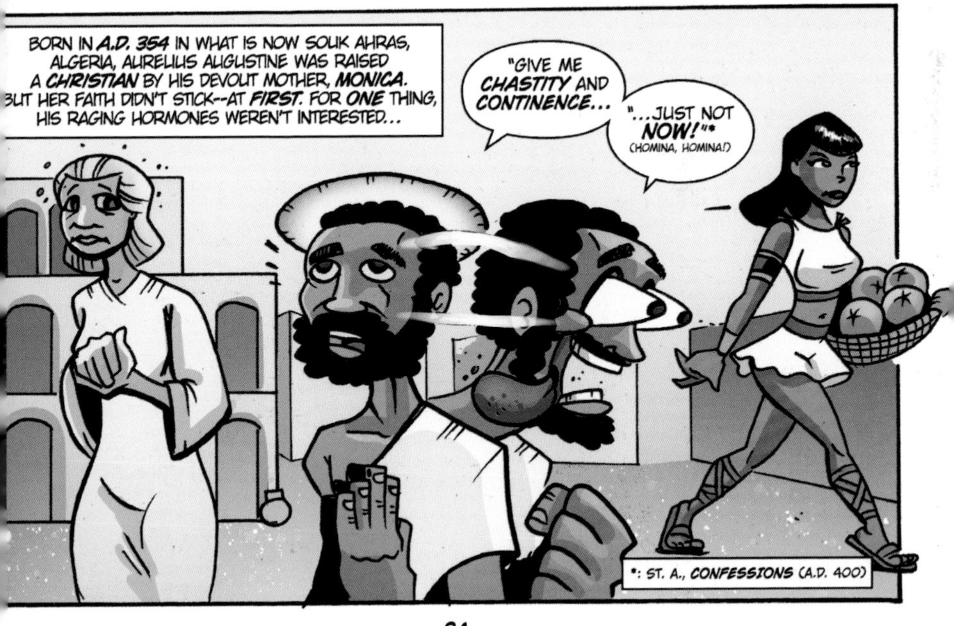
BORN IN A.D. 354 IN WHAT IS NOW SOUK AHRAS, ALGERIA, AURELIUS AUGUSTINE WAS RAISED A CHRISTIAN BY HIS DEVOUT MOTHER, MONICA. BUT HER FAITH DIDN'T STICK--AT FIRST. FOR ONE THING, HIS RAGING HORMONES WEREN'T INTERESTED...
"GIVE ME CHASTITY AND CONTINENCE...
"...JUST NOT NOW!"*
(HOMINA, HOMINA!)
*: ST. A., CONFESSIONS (A.D. 400)

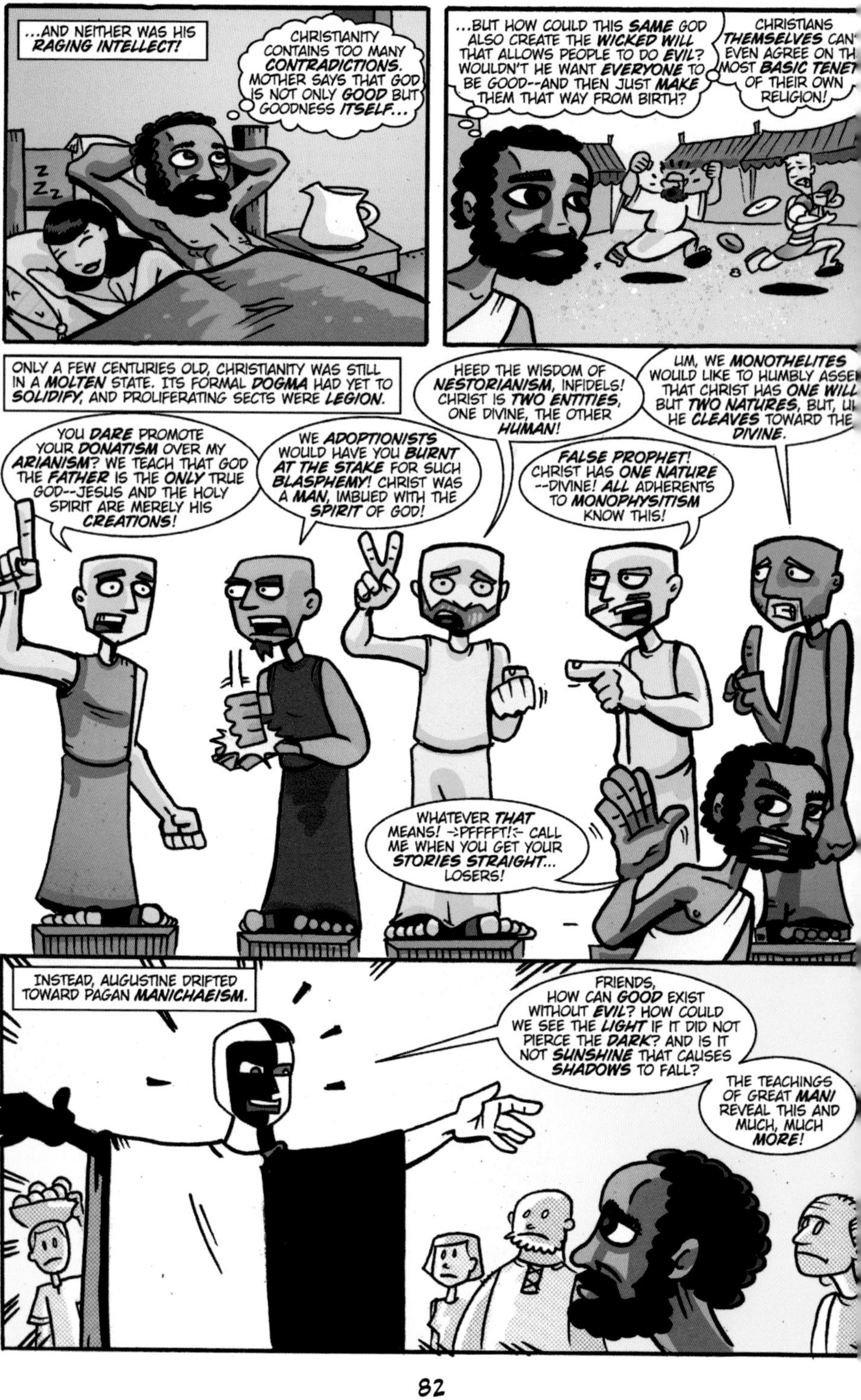
...AND NEITHER WAS HIS RAGING INTELLECT!
CHRISTIANITY CONTAINS TOO MANY CONTRADICTIONS. MOTHER SAYS THAT GOD IS NOT ONLY GOOD BUT GOODNESS ITSELF...
ZZZ
...BUT HOW COULD THIS SAME GOD ALSO CREATE THE WICKED WILL THAT ALLOWS PEOPLE TO DO EVIL? WOULDN'T HE WANT EVERYONE TO BE GOOD--AND THEN JUST MAKE THEM THAT WAY FROM BIRTH?
CHRISTIANS THEMSELVES CAN' EVEN AGREE ON TH MOST BASIC TENET OF THEIR OWN RELIGION!
ONLY A FEW CENTURIES OLD, CHRISTIANITY WAS STILL IN A MOLTEN STATE. ITS FORMAL DOGMA HAD YET TO SOLIDIFY, AND PROLIFERATING SECTS WERE LEGION.
YOU DARE PROMOTE YOUR DONATISM OVER MY ARIANISM? WE TEACH THAT GOD THE FATHER IS THE ONLY TRUE GOD--JESUS AND THE HOLY SPIRIT ARE MERELY HIS CREATIONS!
WE ADOPTIONISTS WOULD HAVE YOU BURNT AT THE STAKE FOR SUCH BLASPHEMY! CHRIST WAS A MAN, IMBUED WITH THE SPIRIT OF GOD!
HEED THE WISDOM OF NESTORIANISM, INFIDELS! CHRIST IS TWO ENTITIES, ONE DIVINE, THE OTHER HUMAN!
FALSE PROPHET! CHRIST HAS ONE NATURE --DIVINE! ALL ADHERENTS TO MONOPHYSITISM KNOW THIS!
UM, WE MONOTHELITES WOULD LIKE TO HUMBLY ASSE THAT CHRIST HAS ONE WILL BUT TWO NATURES, BUT, UI HE CLEAVES TOWARD THE DIVINE.
WHATEVER THAT MEANS! -PFFFFT!- CALL ME WHEN YOU GET YOUR STORIES STRAIGHT... LOSERS!
INSTEAD, AUGUSTINE DRIFTED TOWARD PAGAN MANICHAEISM.
FRIENDS, HOW CAN GOOD EXIST WITHOUT EVIL? HOW COULD WE SEE THE LIGHT IF IT DID NOT PIERCE THE DARK? AND IS IT NOT SUNSHINE THAT CAUSES SHADOWS TO FALL?
THE TEACHINGS OF GREAT MANI REVEAL THIS AND MUCH, MUCH MORE!

THE IRAQI MYSTIC *MANI*, A.K.A. "THE *ILLUSTRIOUS* ONE," SYNTHESIZED VARIOUS KIBBLES & BITS OF BUDDHISM, BABYLONIAN MYTHOLOGY AND ZOROASTRIAN *DUALISM* INTO A PHILOSOPHY THAT SPREAD LIKE *WILDFIRE* THROUGHOUT EUROPE, ASIA AND THE MIDDLE EAST IN THE *THIRD CENTURY*.

HEE HEE HEE

MANI TAUGHT THAT IN THE BEGINNING THE UNIVERSE WAS DIVIDED INTO A REALM OF *LIGHT* AND A REALM OF *DARKNESS*. EACH WAS INFINITE IN *ALL* DIRECTIONS SAVE *ONE*, WHICH WAS WHERE THE TWO REALMS *MET*.

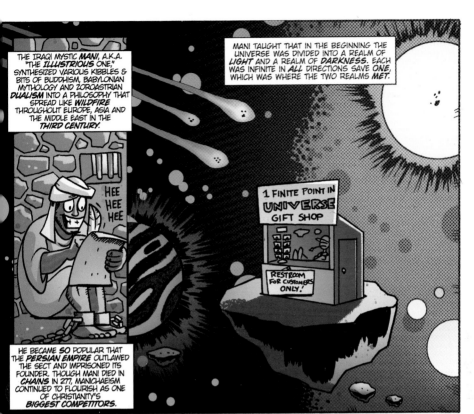

1 FINITE POINT IN UNIVERSE GIFT SHOP

RESTROOM FOR CUSTOMERS ONLY!

HE BECAME *SO* POPULAR THAT THE *PERSIAN EMPIRE* OUTLAWED THE SECT AND IMPRISONED ITS FOUNDER. THOUGH MANI DIED IN *CHAINS* IN 277, MANICHAEISM CONTINUED TO FLOURISH AS ONE OF CHRISTIANITY'S *BIGGEST COMPETITORS*.

ALL MIGHT HAVE REMAINED PEACEFUL IN THIS *"DUOVERSE"* FOREVER, EXCEPT...

MY DARK DOMAIN WOULD BE *PERFECT* NIGHT WERE IT NOT FOR THE *GALLING GLOW* SEEPING IN FROM THE ACCURSED KINGDOM OF LIGHT!

THOOM! THOOM! THOOM!

HARK! THE FEARSOME FOOTFALLS OF THE DARKNESS KING DOTH APPROACH!

THOOM! THOOM! THOOM!

VERILY, A *HERO* MUST RISE AND VANQUISH THE MASTER OF MALFEASANCE BEFORE HE SPOILS MINE LUMINESCENT LAND!

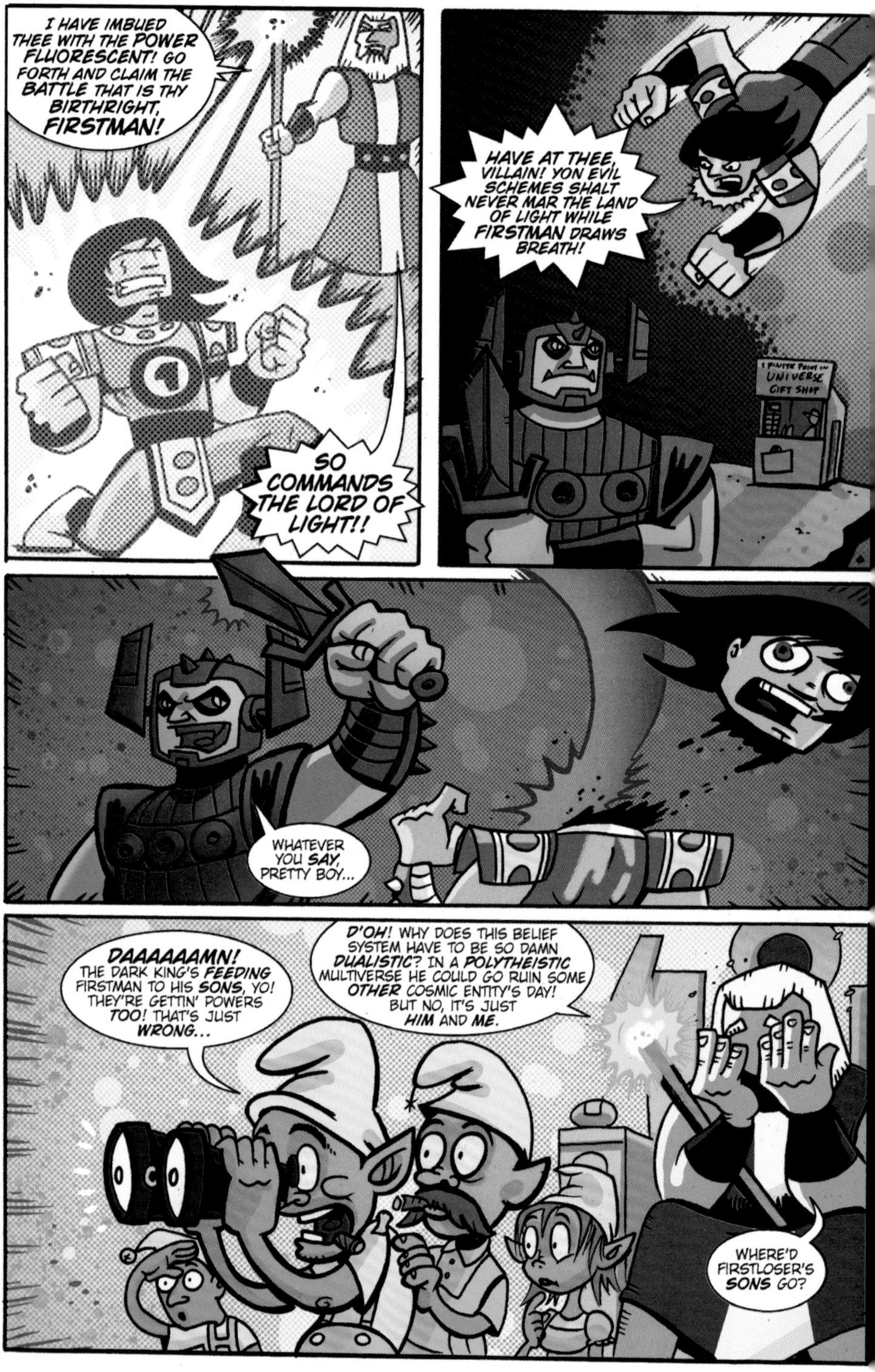
I HAVE IMBUED THEE WITH THE POWER FLUORESCENT! GO FORTH AND CLAIM THE BATTLE THAT IS THY BIRTHRIGHT, FIRSTMAN!
SO COMMANDS THE LORD OF LIGHT!!
HAVE AT THEE, VILLAIN! YON EVIL SCHEMES SHALT NEVER MAR THE LAND OF LIGHT WHILE FIRSTMAN DRAWS BREATH!
UNIVERSE GIFT SHOP
WHATEVER YOU SAY, PRETTY BOY...
DAAAAAAMN! THE DARK KING'S FEEDING FIRSTMAN TO HIS SONS, YO! THEY'RE GETTIN' POWERS TOO! THAT'S JUST WRONG...
D'OH! WHY DOES THIS BELIEF SYSTEM HAVE TO BE SO DAMN DUALISTIC? IN A POLYTHEISTIC MULTIVERSE HE COULD GO RUIN SOME OTHER COSMIC ENTITY'S DAY! BUT NO, IT'S JUST HIM AND ME.
WHERE'D FIRSTLOSER'S SONS GO?

AND SO THE **SONS OF** FIRSTMAN DID BATTLE WITH THEIR DIAMETRIC **OPPOSITES** AMONG THE BROOD OF THE KING OF **DARKNESS.**

CLEAR AIR!

REFRESHING WIND!

BRIGHT LIGHT!

LIFE-GIVING WATERS!

WARMING FIRE!

PESTILENT BREATH!

SCORCHING WIND!

GLOOM!

MIST!

CONSUMING FIRE!

THE SONS OF LIGHT **WON,** AND THE VANQUISHED CORPSES OF THE SONS OF **DARKNESS** BECAME THE MATTER THAT FORMED THE HEAVENS AND THE **EARTH.**

'I FINITE POINT'N! UNIVERSE GIFT SHOP

SINCE **HUMANS** CAME OUT OF THAT **MATTER,** WE'RE MADE OUT OF THE **STUFF** OF DARKNESS--**EVIL!**

BUT DON'T FORGET THAT THE SONS OF DARKNESS *ATE* FIRSTMAN *BEFORE* THEY WERE *SLAUGHTERED*.

SO ALL MATTER-- INCLUDING *HUMANS*-- ARE FESTOONED WITH PARTICLES OF *LIGHT!*

I SEE...SO A MAN MUST KEEP HIS BODY *FREE* OF THE POLLUTION OF *MATTER*, SO HIS *LIGHT PARTICLES* CAN MERGE WITH THE *REALM* OF LIGHT UPON THE BODY'S *DEMISE!*

AUGUSTINE SPENT NINE YEARS AS AN *AUDITOR*, OR "HEARER," AT THE FEET OF THE MANICHEAN *"ELECT"*.

YOU MUST NOT EVER HAVE *CHILDREN!* THAT'S JUST PROMULGATING MORE *MATTER!* IT'S *EVIL!*

NEVER PUT *MEAT* OR *MILK* OR ANYTHING ELSE THAT COMES FROM AN *ANIMAL* INTO YOUR BODY! THAT'S *MATTER!* IT'S *EVIL!*

IN FACT, NEVER HAVE *SEX* AGAIN! HOT, SWEATY *MATTER* ON TOP OF HOT, SWEATY MATTER? THAT'S LIKE A *WAL-MART OF EVIL!!!*

DRAT.

THOUGH HE WAS A *DEVOUT* HEARER, AUGUSTINE'S BRAIN NEVER SHUT ITSELF *OFF*. HE WAS *CONSUMED* BY THE *CONTRADICTIONS* OF HIS FAITH:

THEY SAY THAT ONLY THE *TEETH OF THE ELECT* CAN RELEASE THE *LIGHT* IMPRISONED IN FRUIT, SO WHY DO THE HEARERS HAVE TO EAT IT *TOO?*

NO *NATURAL SCIENTISTS* HAVE EVER FOUND THESE "LIGHT PARTICLES" IN OUR BODIES, SO HOW CAN YOU BE SURE THEY EXIST?

I HAVE NO DOUBT OUR LEARNED BISHOP *FAUSTUS* CAN ANSWER *ALL* YOUR QUESTIONS, AUDITOR!

MANI SAYS THAT PICKING FIGS TO EAT IS TANTAMOUNT TO **SLAYING** THEM AND THEREFORE **EVIL**. SO, TO STAY **PURE**, THE ELECT MUST HAVE THEIR FOOD PICKED **FOR** THEM.

BUT SIMPLE **LOGIC** DICTATES THAT FORCING **OTHERS** TO DO EVIL ON YOUR BEHALF IS ITSELF **EVIL**!

LOOK, YOU SEEM LIKE A **BRIGHT KID**, SO I'M NOT GONNA B.S. YOU: I **CAN'T** EXPLAIN THAT DISCREPANCY...

...BUT SINCE MOST PEOPLE ARE TOO **STUPID** TO UNDERSTAND **HALF** THE STUFF YOU TALK ABOUT, WHO **CARES**? KEEP IT **SIMPLE**: STICK WITH THE GOOD-VERSUS-EVIL STUFF, AND PEOPLE DIE HAPPY ... AND **UNCONFUSED**. YA DIG?

AUGUSTINE WAS SO **DEMORALIZED** BY HIS ENCOUNTER WITH FAUSTUS THAT HE **GAVE UP** BEING A MANICHEAN... IN FACT, HE NEARLY GAVE UP ON **RELIGION** ALTOGETHER!

IN A.D. 383, AUGUSTINE MOVED TO **ITALY** AND BECAME A MUCH SOUGHT-AFTER TEACHER OF **RHETORIC**, INSTRUCTING THE YOUNG **HELLIONS** OF ROMAN ARISTOCRACY HOW TO **TWIST** THE TRUTH TO THEIR ADVANTAGE THROUGH A CUNNING USE OF **LANGUAGE**.

LESSON 1:
HOW to LIE

AS SKILLED AS HE **WAS**, IT WAS STILL A **STRUGGLE**. IT WAS QUITE COMMON IN THOSE DAYS FOR STUDENTS TO **DROP** A CLASS RIGHT BEFORE **TUITION** WAS DUE--

--AND CONTINUE THEIR COURSEWORK WITH **ANOTHER** INSTRUCTOR ACROSS TOWN!

AUGUSTINE'S **HEART** GREW AS EMPTY AS HIS **POCKETBOOK**. IN SEPTEMBER OF 386 HE FOUND HIMSELF IN THE GARDEN OF HIS HOME **DESPAIRING** THAT HIS EXCESSIVELY ANALYTICAL MIND PREVENTED HIM FROM BELIEVING IN **ANYTHING**.

HOW LONG SHALL I GO ON SAYING, "TOMORROW, TOMORROW?" WHY NOT **NOW**? WHY NOT--

WHEN **SUDDENLY**--

TAKE IT AND READ, TAKE IT AND READ...

?

AUGUSTINE LATER WROTE, "WHETHER IT WAS THE VOICE OF A BOY OR A GIRL I CANNOT SAY, BUT AGAIN AND AGAIN IT REPEATED THE REFRAIN:"

TAKE IT AND READ, TAKE IT AND READ...

?

TAKE IT AND READ, TAKE IT AND READ...

NOT IN reveling and drunkenness, not in lust and wantonness, not in quarrels and rivalries. Rather, arm yourselves with the Lord Jesus Christ; spend no more thought on nature and nature's appetites. ROMANS 13:13-14

"IN AN INSTANT, AS I CAME TO THE END OF THE SENTENCE, IT WAS AS THOUGH THE LIGHT OF *CONFIDENCE* FLOODED INTO MY HEART AND ALL THE DARKNESS OF *DOUBT* WAS *DISPELLED*."

AUGUSTINE TOOK THE BIBLE PASSAGE QUITE *LITERALLY.* HE *IMMEDIATELY* GAVE UP HIS JOB "SELLING THE SERVICES OF HIS TONGUE."

LIFETIME CONTRACT

INSTEAD HE PLANNED TO LIVE A LIFE OF *PURE REASON*, IN PURSUIT OF TRUTH. AUGUSTINE RETREATED TO A FRIEND'S COUNTRY ESTATE OUTSIDE *MILAN* WHERE HE HELD *INFORMAL* DEBATE SESSIONS WITH HIS FRIENDS AND RELATIVES--HIS *MOTHER* AMONG THEM!

MY *ERROR* IS SO *OBVIOUS* NOW, MAMA!

I WAS ASKING THE *WRONG QUESTION!* IT IS NOT "WHY IS THERE *EVIL*?"

NO, THE *CORRECT* QUESTION IS...

"WHY IS THERE *GOOD*?"

"GOOD IS JUST ANOTHER WAY OF SAYING 'WHAT GOD WANTS US TO DO.'

BUT ONLY IN EDEN WAS MAN'S FREE WILL PERFECTLY IN SYNCH WITH HIS CREATOR'S-- ADAM'S WANTS WERE THE SAME AS GOD'S!"

"AFTER OUR EXPULSION FROM THE GARDEN, WE BECAME SEPARATED FROM THE LORD. SINCE EVIL IS, IN ESSENCE, THE ABSENCE OF GOD, AFTER OUR FALL FROM GRACE IT BECAME THE MOST COMMON THING ON EARTH!"

"TODAY, ADAM'S SONS AND DAUGHTERS ARE LOST IN MORAL CONFUSION. WE NO LONGER INSTINCTUALLY KNOW THE GOOD."

25¢

"IN FACT, WE CANNOT DO GOOD WITHOUT AN INVITATION FROM GOD-- HIS GRACE, WHICH HE SENDS TO US BECAUSE HE WANTS US TO BE SAVED!"

PLEASE HELP
GOD BLESS

"THOUGH HUMAN WILL IS CAPABLE OF RESISTING GOD'S GRACE, NO ONE EVER DOES. GRACE IS TOO ENTICING TO IGNORE, FOR IT REMINDS US OF OUR ORIGINAL HOME, EDEN!"

BUT IF HUMANITY CANNOT RESIST GRACE, AND IT IS GOD WHO CHOOSES WHO TO GIVE GRACE TO, IT IS THE LORD WHO DECIDES WHO IS SAVED, NOT INDIVIDUAL HUMANS. HOW CAN THAT BE CALLED FREE WILL?

WITH ALL DUE RESPECT, MOTHER, YOU FAIL TO TAKE INTO ACCOUNT AN OBVIOUS POINT:

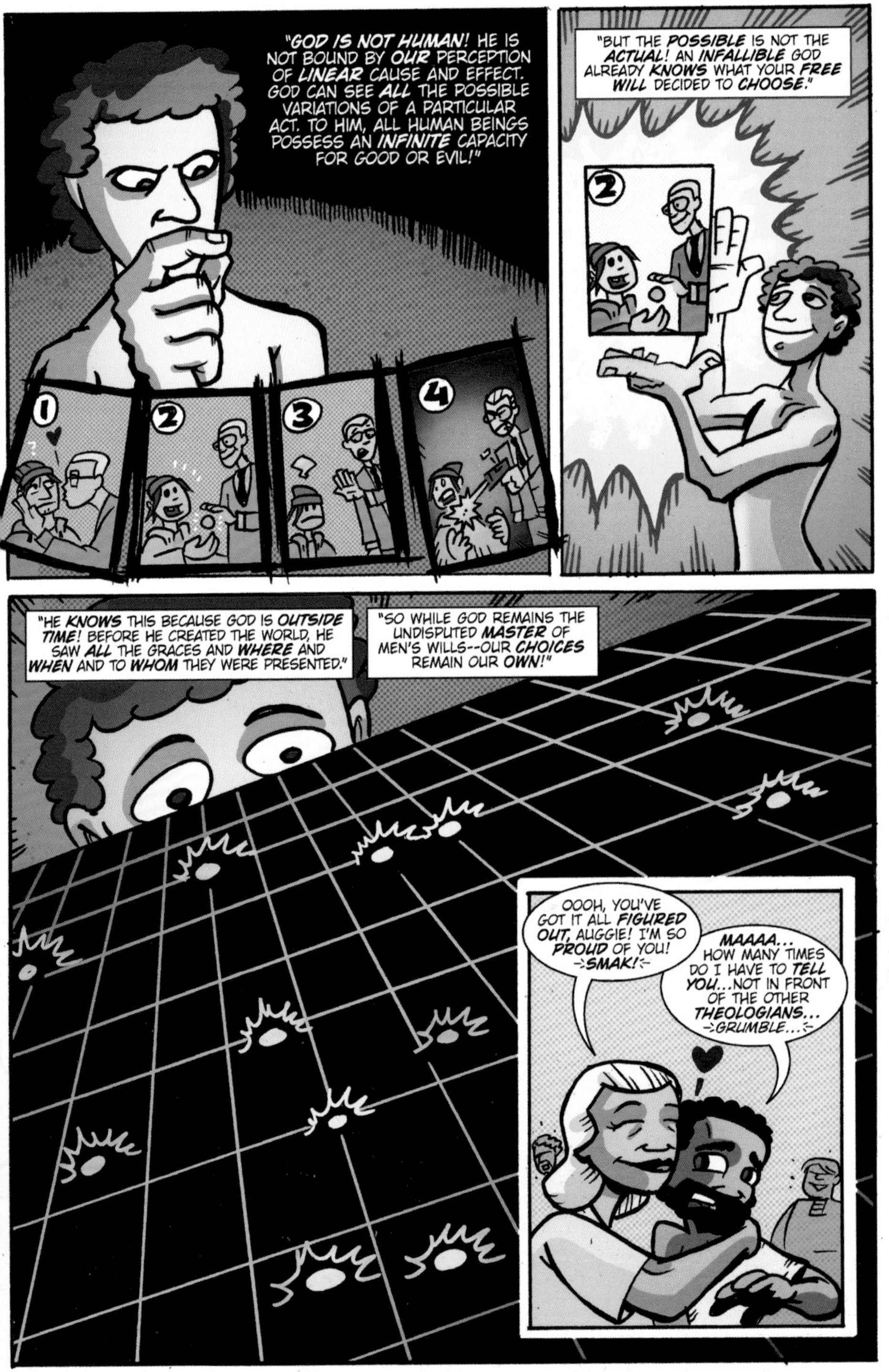
"GOD IS NOT HUMAN! HE IS NOT BOUND BY OUR PERCEPTION OF LINEAR CAUSE AND EFFECT. GOD CAN SEE ALL THE POSSIBLE VARIATIONS OF A PARTICULAR ACT. TO HIM, ALL HUMAN BEINGS POSSESS AN INFINITE CAPACITY FOR GOOD OR EVIL!"
1
2
3
4
"BUT THE POSSIBLE IS NOT THE ACTUAL! AN INFALLIBLE GOD ALREADY KNOWS WHAT YOUR FREE WILL DECIDED TO CHOOSE."
2
"HE KNOWS THIS BECAUSE GOD IS OUTSIDE TIME! BEFORE HE CREATED THE WORLD, HE SAW ALL THE GRACES AND WHERE AND WHEN AND TO WHOM THEY WERE PRESENTED."
"SO WHILE GOD REMAINS THE UNDISPUTED MASTER OF MEN'S WILLS--OUR CHOICES REMAIN OUR OWN!"
OOOH, YOU'VE GOT IT ALL FIGURED OUT, AUGGIE! I'M SO PROUD OF YOU! -SMAK!-
MAAAA... HOW MANY TIMES DO I HAVE TO TELL YOU...NOT IN FRONT OF THE OTHER THEOLOGIANS... -GRUMBLE...-

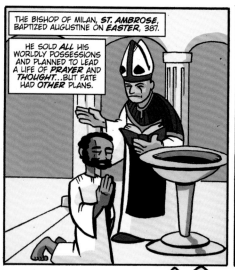

THE BISHOP OF MILAN, *ST. AMBROSE*, BAPTIZED AUGUSTINE ON *EASTER*, 387.

HE SOLD *ALL* HIS WORLDLY POSSESSIONS AND PLANNED TO LEAD A LIFE OF *PRAYER* AND *THOUGHT*...BUT FATE HAD *OTHER* PLANS.

AUGUSTINE'S MOTHER DIED MERE *MONTHS* AFTER HIS BAPTISM. PERHAPS NOT COINCIDENTALLY, SOON THEREAFTER HE RETURNED TO *MOTHER AFRICA*... SPECIFICALLY *HIPPO*, A CITY IN WHAT IS NOW *TUNISIA*.

MONICA WOULD LATER BE *CANONIZED* ALONG WITH HER SON AS THE PATRON SAINT OF *ABUSED WIVES* (AUGGIE'S DAD WAS A *PAGAN*).

ALREADY *FAMOUS* FOR THE WRITINGS THAT HE HAD PRODUCED DURING HIS *SOLITUDE* OUTSIDE MILAN, AUGUSTINE WAS PERSUADED BY THE LOCAL FAITHFUL TO BE *ORDAINED* INTO THE PRIESTHOOD.

IN 396 HE WAS ELECTED *BISHOP OF HIPPO*, THE MOST IMPORTANT SEE IN AFRICA, AN OFFICE HE WOULD HOLD FOR THE NEXT THIRTY-FOUR YEARS!

BISHOP AUGUSTINE SPECIALIZED IN THE ERADICATION OF *HERESY* THROUGH *REASON*. HIS *ORATORICAL SKILLS* QUICKLY BECAME *LEGENDARY*.

AT THE CLIMAX OF HIS DEBATE WITH THE MANICHEAN *FELIX* IN 404, THE ELECT WAS SO *PERSUADED* BY THE BISHOP'S WORDS THAT HE *CONVERTED* ON THE *SPOT!*

HIS SYSTEM OF *DIVINE GRACE* PUT THE KIBOSH ON THE *PELAGIAN* HERESIES, WHICH *DENIED* THE EXISTENCE OF *ORIGINAL SIN!*

THE WINNNNNNNNNAH-- *AUGUSTINE!*

THANKS TO AUGUSTINE'S REASONED EXPLICATION OF THEOLOGY AND DOGMA, THE VARIOUS COMPETING SECTS FELL INTO DISREPAIR, AND THE CHURCH OF ROME THAT THE BISHOP OF HIPPO REPRESENTED--WHICH BECAME KNOWN AS THE *"CATHOLIC"*, OR *"UNIVERSAL"* CHURCH, GREW EVER STRONGER!

MANICHEANISM

CONVERTED TO CATHOLIC

CONDEMNED

AUGUSTINE BATTLED HERESY *LITERALLY* TO HIS DYING DAYS. AS HE LAY DYING IN 430, THE *VANDALS*, ADHERENTS OF *ARIANISM* (SEE PG. 60), WERE *LAYING SIEGE* TO HIPPO!

AUGGIE SUCKS

ONE OF THE MOST *PROLIFIC* THINKERS EVER, AUGUSTINE REFUTED COMPETING SECTS LIKE THE *DONATISTS* (WHICH HELD THAT ONLY THE *MORALLY PURE* COULD BECOME *PRIESTS*) WITH OVER *ONE THOUSAND SEPARATE WORKS* ON CHRISTIAN THOUGHT AND CHURCH DOCTRINE!

OHHHH...!!

AFTER HIS CANONIZATION, HE BECAME THE PATRON SAINT OF *BREWERS* (FOR HIS FORMERLY WILD WAYS) AND, OF COURSE, *THEOLOGIANS...*

...BUT MOST *IMPORTANTLY*, HE IS KNOWN AS THE *GREATEST* OF THE CHURCH *FATHERS*. HIS *FEAST DAY* IS *AUGUST 28TH*.

NOW MARY, CAN YOU *EXPLAIN* WHAT WE *LEARNED* TODAY?

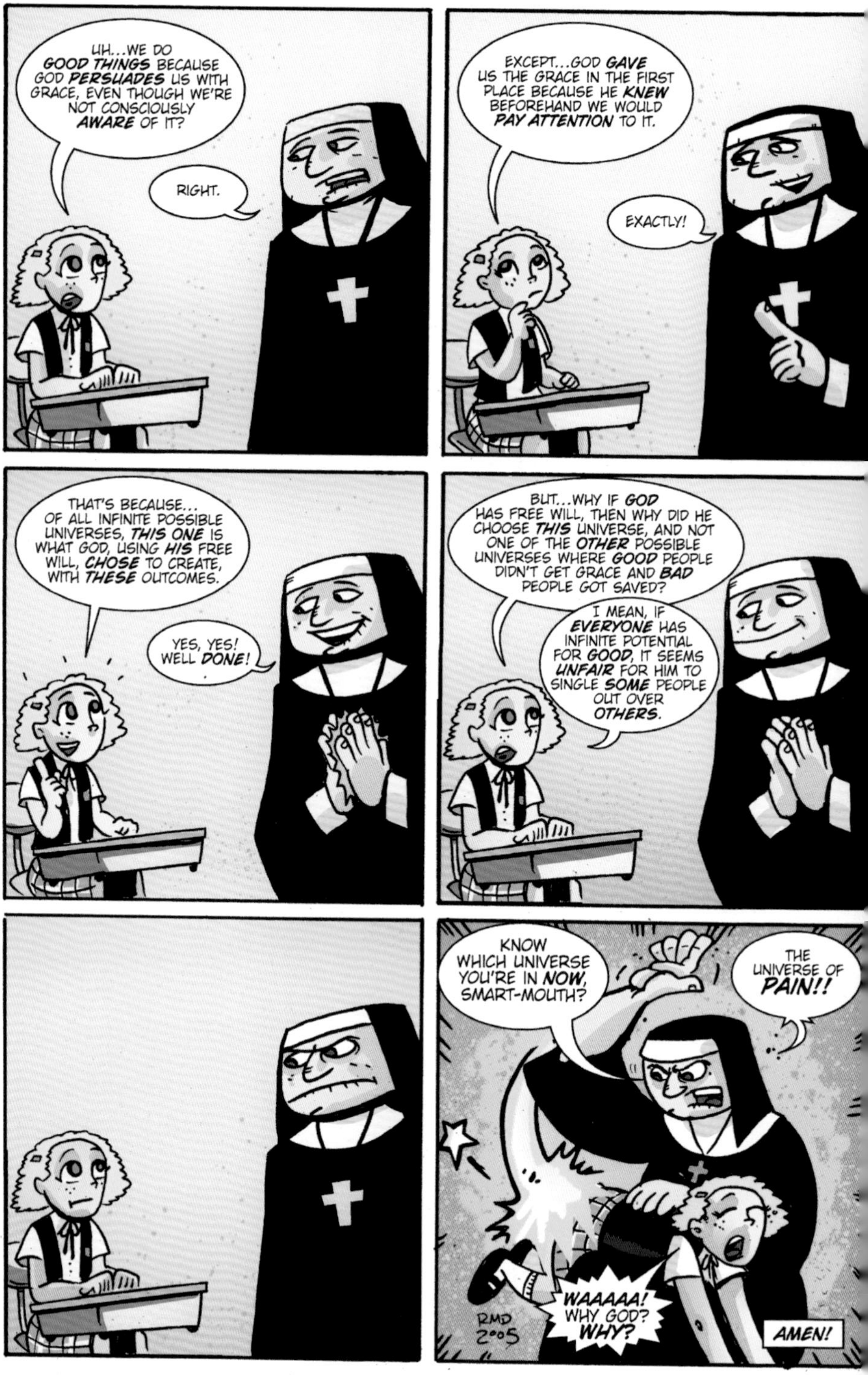
UH...WE DO GOOD THINGS BECAUSE GOD PERSUADES US WITH GRACE, EVEN THOUGH WE'RE NOT CONSCIOUSLY AWARE OF IT?
RIGHT.
EXCEPT...GOD GAVE US THE GRACE IN THE FIRST PLACE BECAUSE HE KNEW BEFOREHAND WE WOULD PAY ATTENTION TO IT.
EXACTLY!
THAT'S BECAUSE... OF ALL INFINITE POSSIBLE UNIVERSES, THIS ONE IS WHAT GOD, USING HIS FREE WILL, CHOSE TO CREATE, WITH THESE OUTCOMES.
YES, YES! WELL DONE!
BUT...WHY IF GOD HAS FREE WILL, THEN WHY DID HE CHOOSE THIS UNIVERSE, AND NOT ONE OF THE OTHER POSSIBLE UNIVERSES WHERE GOOD PEOPLE DIDN'T GET GRACE AND BAD PEOPLE GOT SAVED?
I MEAN, IF EVERYONE HAS INFINITE POTENTIAL FOR GOOD, IT SEEMS UNFAIR FOR HIM TO SINGLE SOME PEOPLE OUT OVER OTHERS.
KNOW WHICH UNIVERSE YOU'RE IN NOW, SMART-MOUTH?
THE UNIVERSE OF PAIN!!
WAAAAA! WHY GOD? WHY?
RMD 2005
AMEN!

Our hunger to under-
stand the *world*, to
know why and how and
what the essential
nature of things are
has been a part of each
one of *us* from our
earliest days.

And so it was in
the early days
of *humanity* as
a whole.

Even in *ancient* times,
people observed the
workings of nature
and wrote down what
they *saw*.

To *pre*historic
peoples, *eclipses*
might have been
terrifying--
looking like a
giant dragon
devouring
the *sun*--

GAHHH! THE
WORLD CAN'T
END! WE JUST
INVENTED FIRE
YESTERDAY!

*I CAN SEE
WHAT'S INSIDE
CAVES NOW!*

--but not for *long.*

SO...WE HAVE REACHED THE *MAXIMUM* PHASE OF THE ECLIPSE, AT...*CAPRICORN SIX.*

MAKE A *NOTE* OF IT, HYPATIA.

CAPRICON SIX. *GOT* IT, FATHER.

NOW REMEMBER, GIRL, WHAT *DON'T* WE DO?

LOOK DIRECTLY AT THE SUN.

AND WHY DON'T WE DO THAT?

YOU'LL *BURN YOUR EYES OUT!*

HA, HA. YES, QUITE.

Humanity's scientific knowledge was so good by AD 364 that *Theon of Alexandria* was able to predict a solar *and* a lunar eclipse.

THEON! YOU CAN PREDICT ECLIPSES BUT CAN YOU TELL ME THE NAME OF THE *MAN* I'LL MARRY?

HA HA, I AM AFRAID IT DOESN'T *WORK* THAT WAY, MADAM...

THEON! WHAT ARE MY WINNING *LOTTO NUMBERS?!*

96

Theon was considered the greatest mathematician and scientist of his day, but even *he* said he was surpassed by his *daughter*...

HYPATIA!
THE LAST OF THE FIRSTS!

Our story begins in Africa, in Egypt's Greek colony of Alexandria, then the center of learning for the Roman Empire, and therefore the Western world.

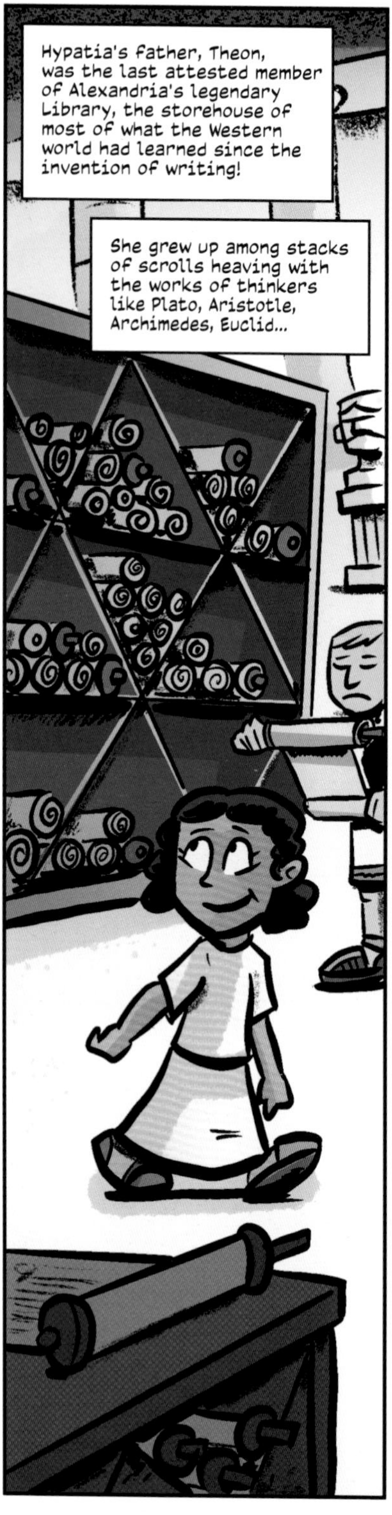
Hypatia's father, Theon, was the last attested member of Alexandria's legendary Library, the storehouse of most of what the Western world had learned since the invention of writing!
She grew up among stacks of scrolls heaving with the works of thinkers like Plato, Aristotle, Archimedes, Euclid...

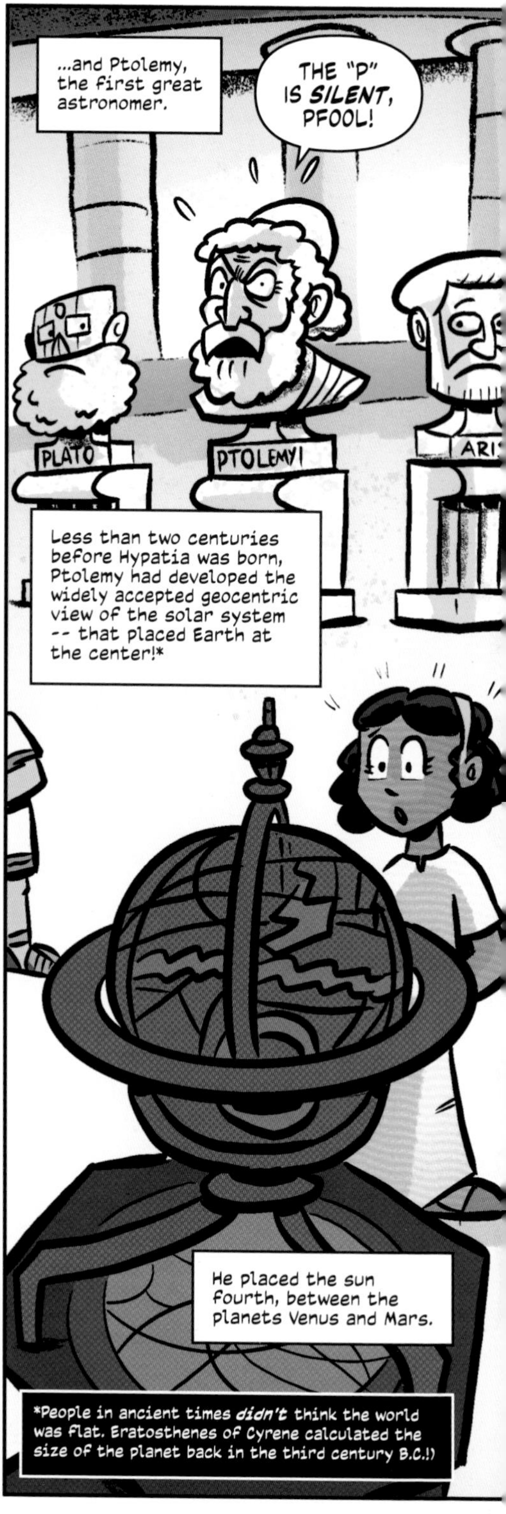
...and Ptolemy, the first great astronomer.
THE "P" IS ***SILENT***, PFOOL!
PLATO
PTOLEMY
ARI
Less than two centuries before Hypatia was born, Ptolemy had developed the widely accepted geocentric view of the solar system -- that placed Earth at the center!*
He placed the sun fourth, between the planets Venus and Mars.
*People in ancient times ***didn't*** think the world was flat. Eratosthenes of Cyrene calculated the size of the planet back in the third century B.C.!)

In those days, science was considered a branch of *mathematics*--along with *music*, but that's another story entirely!

Astronomy is a *practical* application of math because its objects are *physical*--like sun, moon, planets-- and you can use it to build clocks and calendars and aid in navigation.

So while Ptolemy and Theon and, later, *Hypatia* would have been called *mathematicians* instead of scientists in their day, she really became a *Jane* of all trades!

As an adult, Hypatia spoke and wrote on philosophy, religion, arithmetic, and geometry as well as astronomy.

But her primary fame came from her skill as a *teacher*-- her inspirational skills became legendary!

HOW DOES SCIENCE WORK?

THROUGH A COMBINATION OF *OBSERVATION* AND *ABSTRACTION.*

YOU GATHER DATA OBJECTIVELY UNTIL IT FORMS A *PATTERN*, THEN YOU SEE IF YOU CAN *PREDICT* THINGS *USING* THAT PATTERN.

IF YOU *CAN*, THAT MEANS YOU GOT IT *RIGHT!*

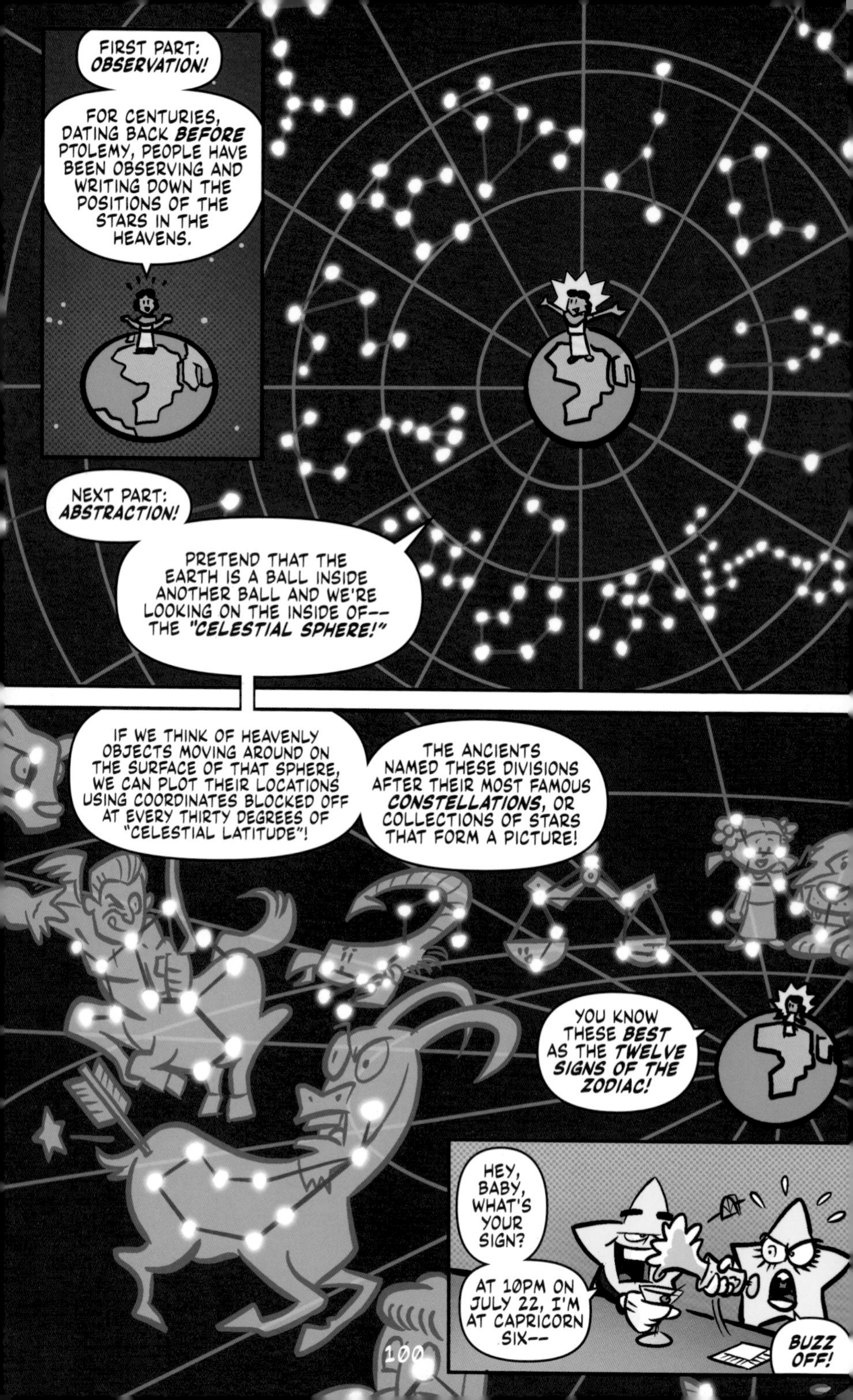
FIRST PART: OBSERVATION!
FOR CENTURIES, DATING BACK BEFORE PTOLEMY, PEOPLE HAVE BEEN OBSERVING AND WRITING DOWN THE POSITIONS OF THE STARS IN THE HEAVENS.
NEXT PART: ABSTRACTION!
PRETEND THAT THE EARTH IS A BALL INSIDE ANOTHER BALL AND WE'RE LOOKING ON THE INSIDE OF-- THE "CELESTIAL SPHERE!"
IF WE THINK OF HEAVENLY OBJECTS MOVING AROUND ON THE SURFACE OF THAT SPHERE, WE CAN PLOT THEIR LOCATIONS USING COORDINATES BLOCKED OFF AT EVERY THIRTY DEGREES OF "CELESTIAL LATITUDE"!
THE ANCIENTS NAMED THESE DIVISIONS AFTER THEIR MOST FAMOUS CONSTELLATIONS, OR COLLECTIONS OF STARS THAT FORM A PICTURE!
YOU KNOW THESE BEST AS THE TWELVE SIGNS OF THE ZODIAC!
HEY, BABY, WHAT'S YOUR SIGN?
AT 10PM ON JULY 22, I'M AT CAPRICORN SIX--
BUZZ OFF!

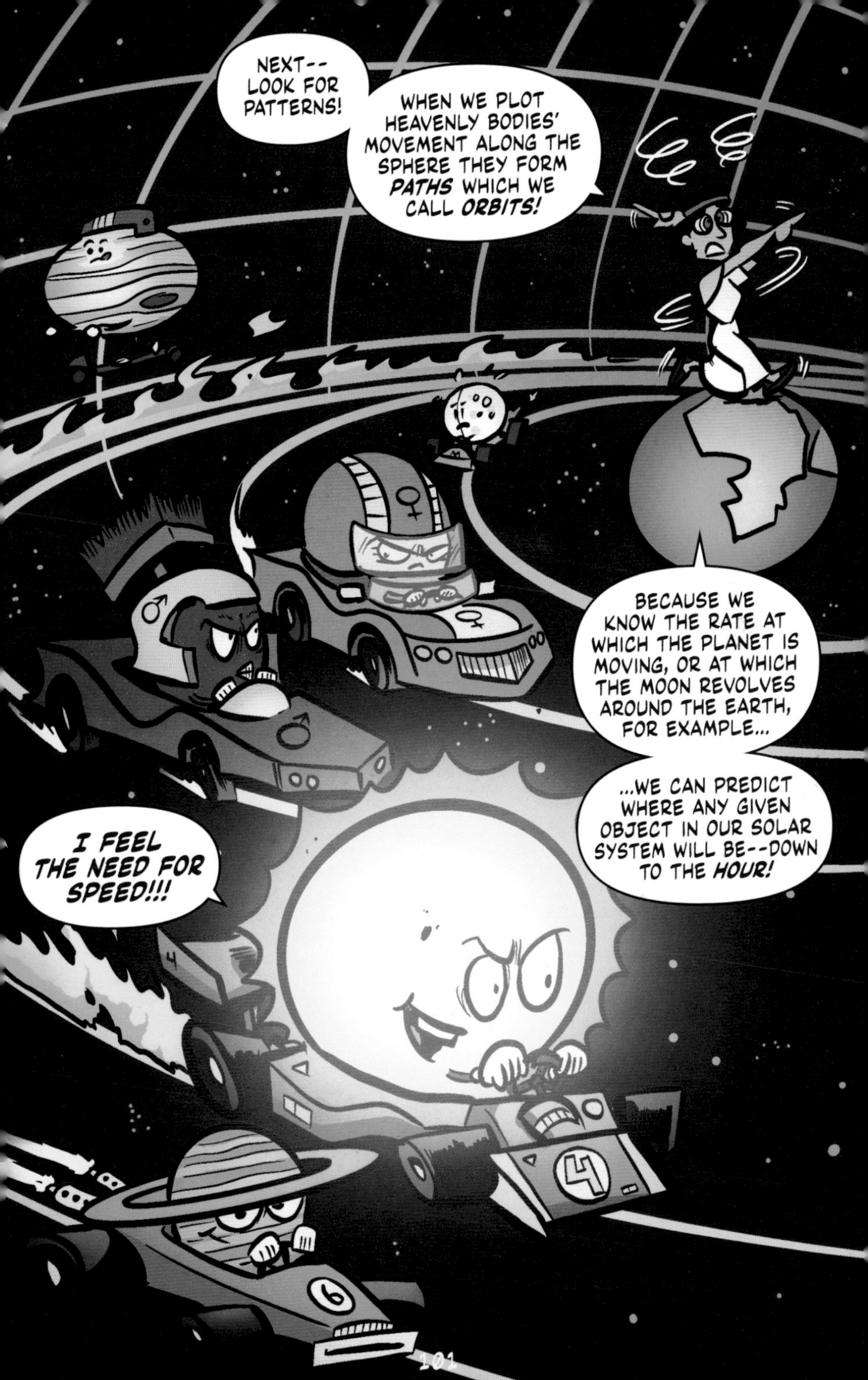
NEXT--
LOOK FOR
PATTERNS!
WHEN WE PLOT HEAVENLY BODIES' MOVEMENT ALONG THE SPHERE THEY FORM *PATHS* WHICH WE CALL *ORBITS!*
BECAUSE WE KNOW THE RATE AT WHICH THE PLANET IS MOVING, OR AT WHICH THE MOON REVOLVES AROUND THE EARTH, FOR EXAMPLE...
...WE CAN PREDICT WHERE ANY GIVEN OBJECT IN OUR SOLAR SYSTEM WILL BE--DOWN TO THE *HOUR!*
I FEEL THE NEED FOR SPEED!!!

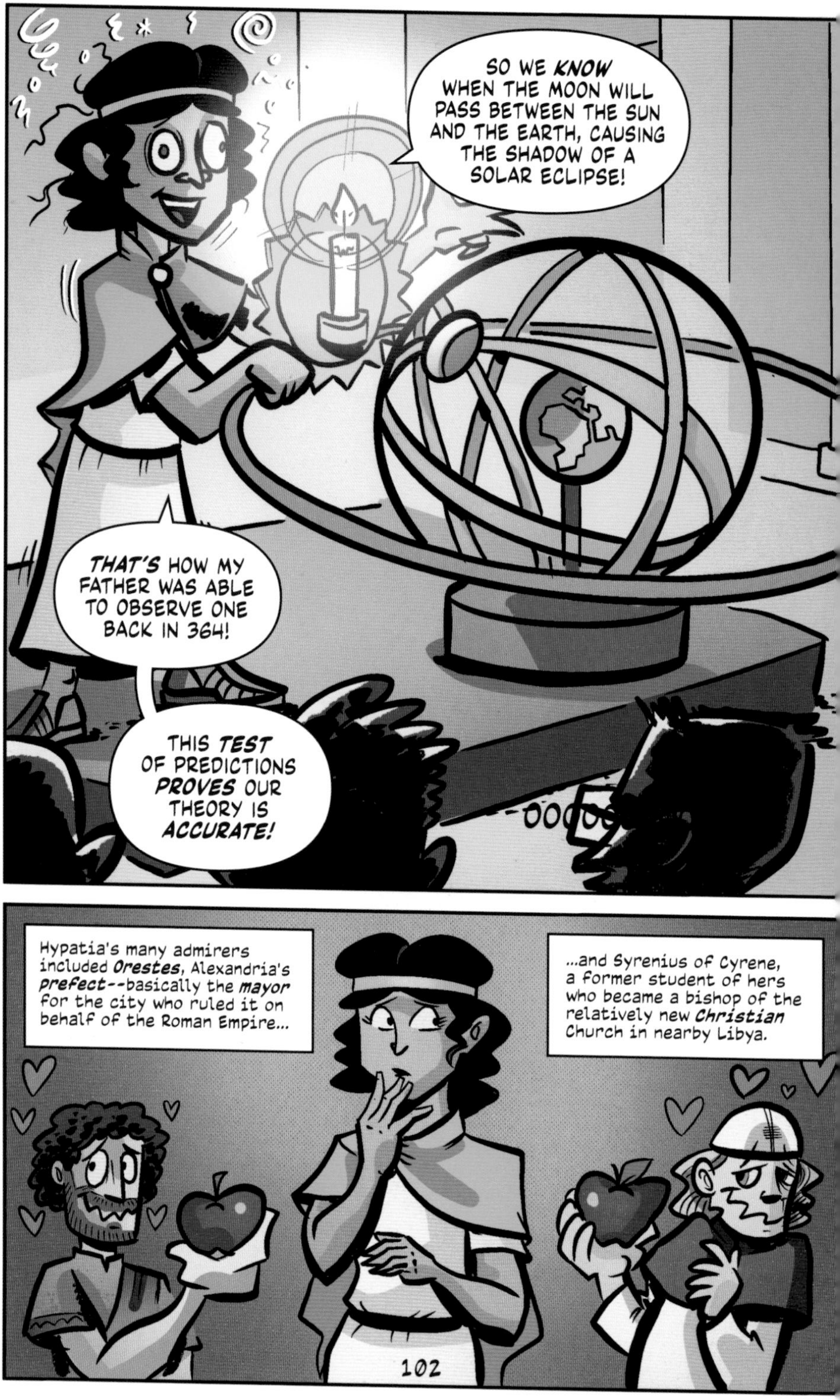
SO WE KNOW WHEN THE MOON WILL PASS BETWEEN THE SUN AND THE EARTH, CAUSING THE SHADOW OF A SOLAR ECLIPSE!
THAT'S HOW MY FATHER WAS ABLE TO OBSERVE ONE BACK IN 364!
THIS TEST OF PREDICTIONS PROVES OUR THEORY IS ACCURATE!
Hypatia's many admirers included Orestes, Alexandria's prefect--basically the mayor for the city who ruled it on behalf of the Roman Empire...
...and Syrenius of Cyrene, a former student of hers who became a bishop of the relatively new Christian Church in nearby Libya.

Syrenius did not believe his *faith* interfered with his love of *science*.

Together, he and Hypatia crafted a cutting-edge silver *astrolabe* to further astronomical calculations.

This device is essentially the celestial sphere *flattened* into a group of movable discs...

...through which one may tell time, find stars and planets, their altitude, and where they rise in the night sky.

Hypatia used this data gleaned through the astrolabe to improve Ptolemy's ancient star charts to the point where even Theon admitted his daughter's skill had far exceeded his own!

When Theon passed away, Hypatia inherited his mantle as the greatest scientist and mathematician in the world!

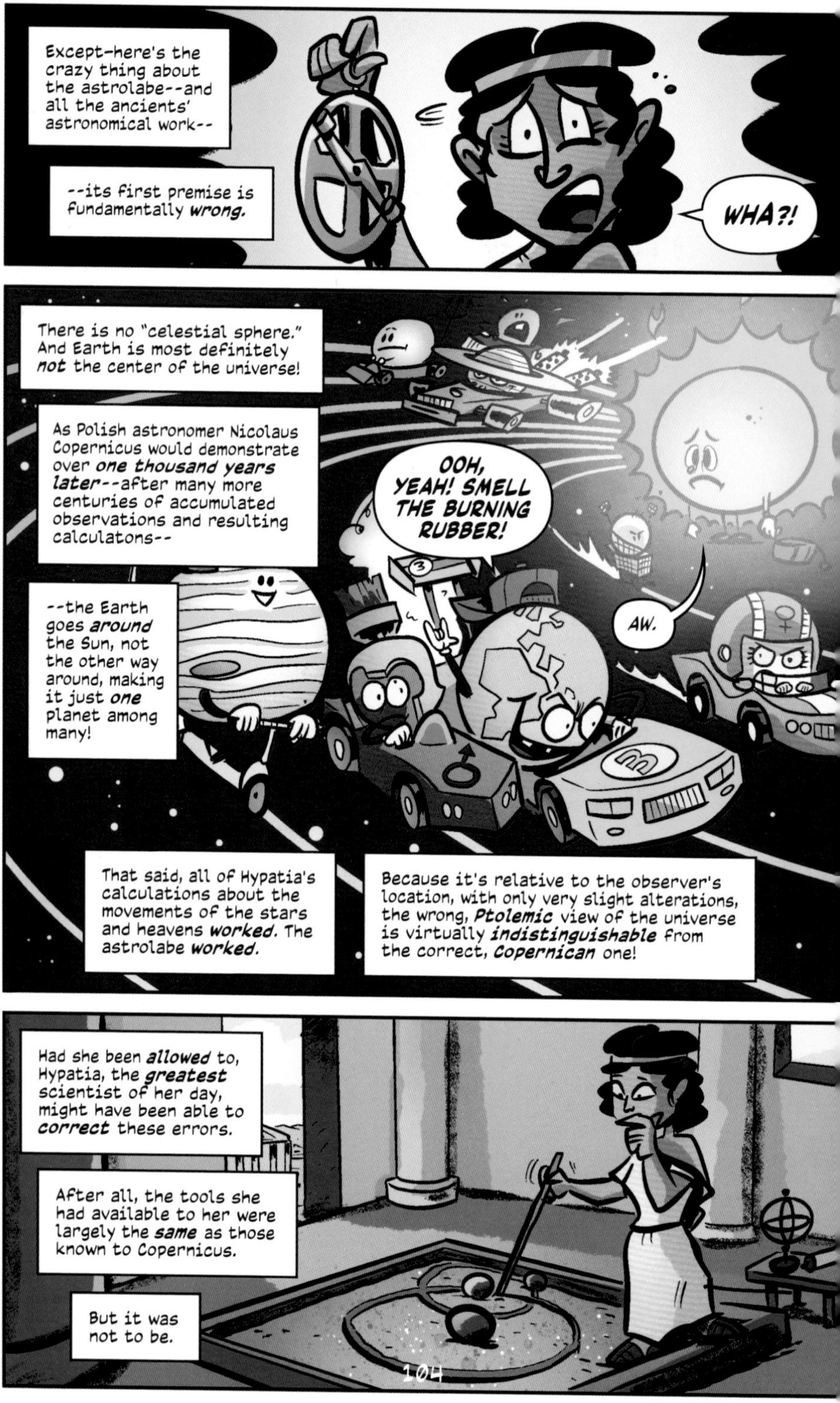

Except--here's the crazy thing about the astrolabe--and all the ancients' astronomical work--
--its first premise is fundamentally *wrong.*
WHA?!
There is no "celestial sphere." And Earth is most definitely *not* the center of the universe!
As Polish astronomer Nicolaus Copernicus would demonstrate over *one thousand years later*--after many more centuries of accumulated observations and resulting calculatons--
OOH, YEAH! SMELL THE BURNING RUBBER!
--the Earth goes *around* the Sun, not the other way around, making it just *one* planet among many!
AW.
That said, all of Hypatia's calculations about the movements of the stars and heavens *worked*. The astrolabe *worked*.
Because it's relative to the observer's location, with only very slight alterations, the wrong, *Ptolemic* view of the universe is virtually *indistinguishable* from the correct, *Copernican* one!
Had she been *allowed* to, Hypatia, the *greatest* scientist of her day, might have been able to *correct* these errors.
After all, the tools she had available to her were largely the *same* as those known to Copernicus.
But it was not to be.

Cyril, the bishop of Alexandria, wanted to drive all non-Christians out of the city, particularly the Jews--but the Roman prefect, Hypatia's friend Orestes, resisted.

It was widely believed that the prefect's close advisor, *Hypatia*, had counseled moderation.

Hypatia's student and collaborator Bishop Synesius died suddenly in AD 413, leaving her, a non-Christian teaching outside the confines of the Church, a politically *vulnerable* target.

In AD 415 a mob of fanatics dragged her from her carriage...

SHE'S AN ASTROLOGER AND A WITCH! SHE KNOWS WHEN ECLIPSES HAPPEN! SHE CAN PREDICT THE FUTURE!

TELL ME MY HOROSCOPE! WILL I RECEIVE UNEXPECTED BENEFITS FROM A NEW FRIEND?!

YOU STILL HAVEN'T TOLD ME MY WINNING LOTTO NUMBERS!

...and stoned her to death inside their church.

UH...IT SAYS RIGHT HERE *"THOU SHALT NOT KILL"*...

SEEMS NOT REALLY, Y'KNOW, A *SUGGESTION*...

Bishop Cyril claimed he had no involvement in the attack, but he soon got his way and Alexandria was purged of all other faiths... other ways of *thinking*.

The Library at Alexandria closed for good, and much of the knowledge that it stored --including all of *Hypatia's* writings--*burned*.

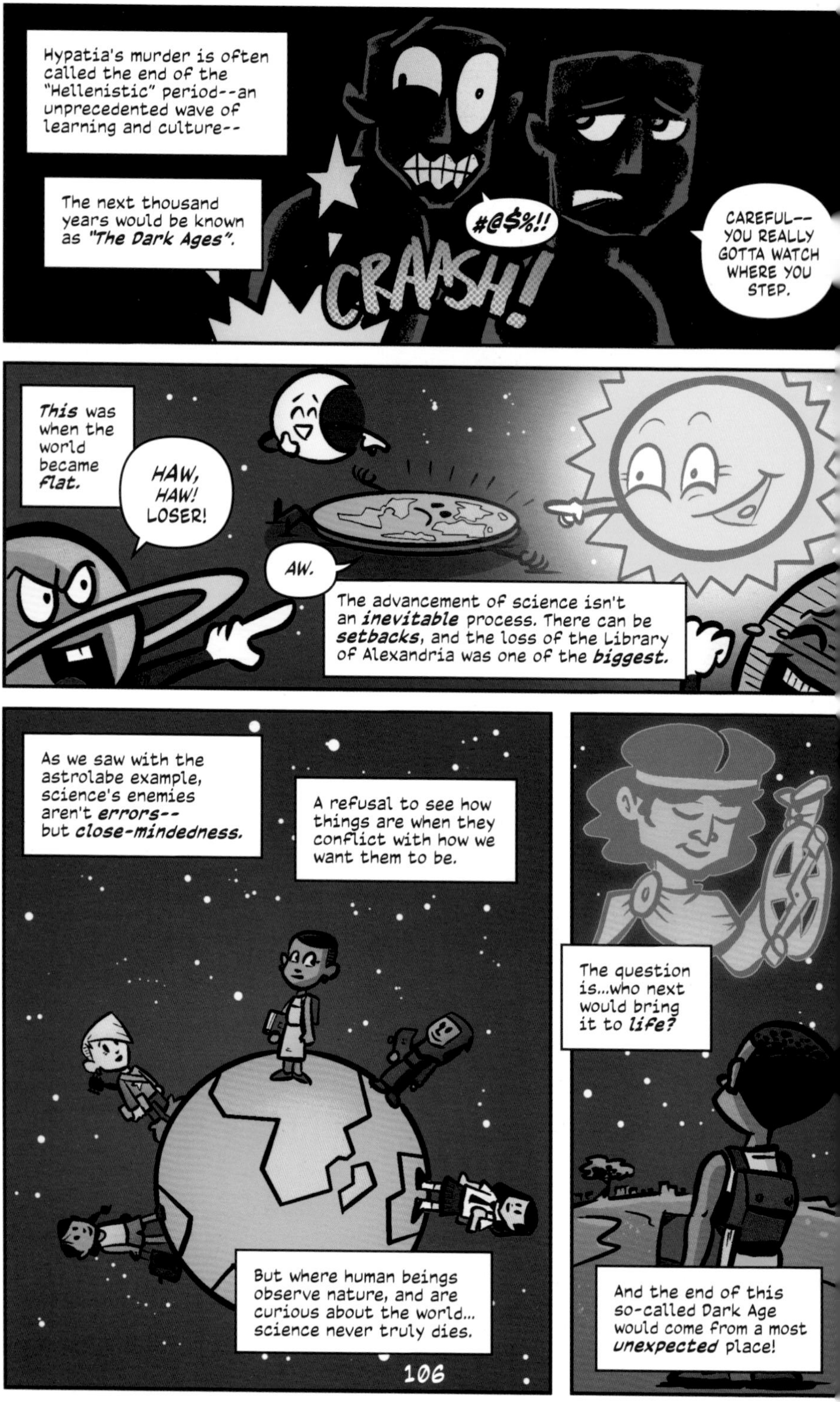
Hypatia's murder is often called the end of the "Hellenistic" period--an unprecedented wave of learning and culture--
The next thousand years would be known as *"The Dark Ages"*.
#@$%!!
CRAASH!
CAREFUL--
YOU REALLY GOTTA WATCH WHERE YOU STEP.
This was when the world became *flat.*
HAW, HAW! LOSER!
AW.
The advancement of science isn't an ***inevitable*** process. There can be ***setbacks***, and the loss of the Library of Alexandria was one of the ***biggest.***
As we saw with the astrolabe example, science's enemies aren't ***errors--*** but ***close-mindedness.***
A refusal to see how things are when they conflict with how we want them to be.
But where human beings observe nature, and are curious about the world... science never truly dies.
The question is...who next would bring it to ***life?***
And the end of this so-called Dark Age would come from a most ***unexpected*** place!

LOOK OUT, ATHEISTS!!

HERE COMES *THREE HUNDRED POUNDS* OF THEOLOGICAL THAUMATURGY...

THAT *PEERLESS PACHYDERM* OF *PIOUS POSTULATING*...

THE MAN THEY CALL THE "*SCHOLASTIC SPASTIC*"...

(*...AND ACTION PHILOSOPHER #17!*)

St. Thomas Aquinas!

LIKE A *LOT* OF PARENTS, THE COUNT OF AQUINO WAS LESS THAN *THRILLED* WHEN HE LEARNED THAT HIS SON HAD SWITCHED *MAJORS* MIDWAY THROUGH HIS *COLLEGE CAREER*.

WHAT? YOU WANT TO JOIN THE DOMINICANS? OVER MY DEAD BODY!!

I DIDN'T PAY FOR FOUR YEARS AT THE *UNIVERSITY OF NAPLES* FOR YOU TO TAKE A VOW OF *POVERTY* AND *HUMILITY!*

I'M *SORRY*, FATHER, BUT I'VE MADE UP MY *MIND*.

THEN I SHALL GIVE YOU *PLENTY* OF TIME TO *CHANGE* IT!

GUARDS! THROW HIM IN THE *TOWER!*

I AM TOLD YOU ARE THE *GREATEST* PROSTITUTE IN *ALL* OF ITALY!

YES. YES I AM.

YOU *MUST* SEDUCE MY SON INTO *BREAKING* THE VOWS OF HIS *ORDER!*

HOW ELSE CAN HE BECOME POPE?!

THE COUNT INSTALLED THE TEMPTRESS IN THOMAS'S ROOM IN THE FORTRESS OF *SAN GIOVANNI* AT *ROCCO SECCA.*

OOOHHHH TOOOOMMMMEEE...

I NEED *HELP* REMOVING ALL THIS TIGHT, RESTRICTING *LINGERIE...*

OH, GOLLY, SHE'S SO *HOT!* WHAT AM I GONNA DO, LORD?!?

Fear NOT Thomas! God has HEARD thy prayers and sent US to help thee!

Did not a HOLY MAN on the hour of thy birth predict that NO ONE would be found to equal to thy LEARNING and thy SANCTITY?

We GIRD THEE with the girdle of PERPETUAL VIRGINITY!

AWESOME! GOD'S THE *BEST!*

Yes. We know. We're ANGELS.

108

~HEH, HEH!~ ONCE THAT WILY STRUMPET STAINS THOMAS'S CHASTITY **BEYOND REDEMPTION,** THE DOMINICANS WILL HAVE NO **CHOICE** BUT TO BOOT HIS ASS RIGHT OUT OF THE ORDER!

THEN HE'LL BE FREE TO BECOME THE BISHOP OR **CARDINAL** I ALWAYS **WANTED**...

FAT **VATICAN CONTRACTS,** HERE I **COME**...

EEEEEEEEE!!

BACK TO THE DEPTHS OF THE **INFERNO** WITH YOU, **HELLSPAWN!!**

THOMAS'S PARENTS HELD HIM IN CAPTIVITY FOR NEARLY **TWO YEARS**.

FINALLY, AROUND **1245,** THE COUNTESS PERSUADED HER HUSBAND TO LET THEIR SON FOLLOW WHAT HE CLEARLY SAW AS **GOD'S WILL.**

HE WAS LOWERED DOWN TO HIS BROTHER MONKS IN A **BASKET.**

SPLAT!

(WE CAN ONLY ASSUME THE BASKET WAS THE **COUNT'S** IDEA.)

HE DOMINICANS DISCOVERED THOMAS HAD SPENT HIS IMPRISONMENT **STUDYING,** SO THEY SENT HIM TO **PARIS,** THE CENTER OF **LEARNING** OF THE MEDIEVAL WORLD.

MANY OF HIS TEACHERS MISTOOK HIS EXTREME HUMILITY FOR **DULLNESS,** CALLING HIM A "DUMB OX", BUT LEGENDARY THEOLOGIAN **ALBERT THE GREAT** RECOGNIZED:

THAT "DUMB OX'S" BELLOWING IN **DOCTRINE** WILL ONE DAY RESOUND THROUGH-OUT THE **WORLD!**

ALBERT BELIEVED THAT FAITH SHOULD BE MARRIED TO *REASON* WHENEVER POSSIBLE!

HE LED THE *"SCHOLASTIC"* MOVEMENT THAT FUSED CHRISTIAN TEACHINGS WITH THE NEWLY-TRANSLATED (INTO *LATIN*) SECULAR PHILOSOPHIES OF *ARISTOTLE*!

HEY! LOOK WHAT *I* FOUND!

WHEN THOMAS BEGAN TEACHING IN PARIS *HIMSELF* IN *1252*, HE WAS OPPOSED, AT FIRST, BY *PLATONISTS* (LIKE *ST. BONAVENTURA*) WHO FELT ARISTOTLE'S *REJECTION* OF THE THEORY OF FORMS DENIED THAT GOD POSSESSED ALL THE *IDEAS* OF THE WORLD!

THOMAS SET ABOUT *"CHRISTIANIZING"* ARISTOTLE TO MAKE HIM FIT FOR USE IN THE *THEOLOGICAL* CLASSROOM!

HE WROTE IN CAREFULLY-CONSTRUCTED *DIALECTICS* THAT EXEMPLIFIED THE CLEAR, SIMPLE STRUCTURE OF ARISTOTELIAN *LOGIC*:

QUESTION: Whether God exists?

OBJECTION: IT SEEMS THAT GOD DOES *NOT* EXIST; FOR THE WORD "GOD" MEANS THAT HE IS *INFINITE GOODNESS*.

IF, THEREFORE, GOD *EXISTED*, THERE WOULD BE NO *EVIL* DISCOVERABLE; BUT THERE *IS* EVIL IN THE WORLD.

THEREFORE, GOD DOES *NOT* EXIST!

ON *THE CONTRARY*, IT IS SAID IN THE PERSON OF GOD: *"I AM WHO I AM"* (EXODUS 3:14).

I ANSWER THAT, THE EXISTENCE OF GOD CAN BE PROVED IN *FIVE* WAYS:

Proof the First: from MOTION

IT IS CERTAIN, AND EVIDENT TO OUR SENSES, THAT IN THE WORLD SOME THINGS ARE IN MOTION.

NOW WHATEVER IS IN MOTION IS PUT IN MOTION BY ANOTHER, FOR NOTHING CAN BE IN MOTION EXCEPT IT IS IN POTENTIALITY TO THAT TOWARDS WHICH IT IS IN MOTION.

FOR MOTION IS NOTHING ELSE THAN THE REDUCTION OF SOMETHING FROM POTENTIALITY TO ACTUALITY.

POTENTIAL   ACTUAL

BUT NOTHING CAN BE REDUCED FROM POTENTIALITY TO ACTUALITY, EXCEPT BY SOMETHING IN A STATE OF ACTUALITY!

IT IS THEREFORE IMPOSSIBLE THAT A THING SHOULD BE MOVER AND MOVED, I.E. THAT IT SHOULD MOVE ITSELF!

IF THAT BY WHICH IT IS PUT IN MOTION BE ITSELF PUT IN MOTION, THEN THIS ALSO MUST NEEDS BE PUT IN MOTION BY ANOTHER, AND THAT BY ANOTHER AGAIN...

...BUT THIS CANNOT GO ON TO INFINITY, BECAUSE THEN THERE WOULD BE NO FIRST MOVER, AND, CONSEQUENTLY NO OTHER MOVER.

THEREFORE IT IS NECESSARY TO ARRIVE AT A FIRST MOVER, PUT IN MOTION BY NO OTHER...

...AND THIS EVERYONE UNDERSTANDS TO BE GOD!

Proof the Second: from EFFICIENT CAUSE

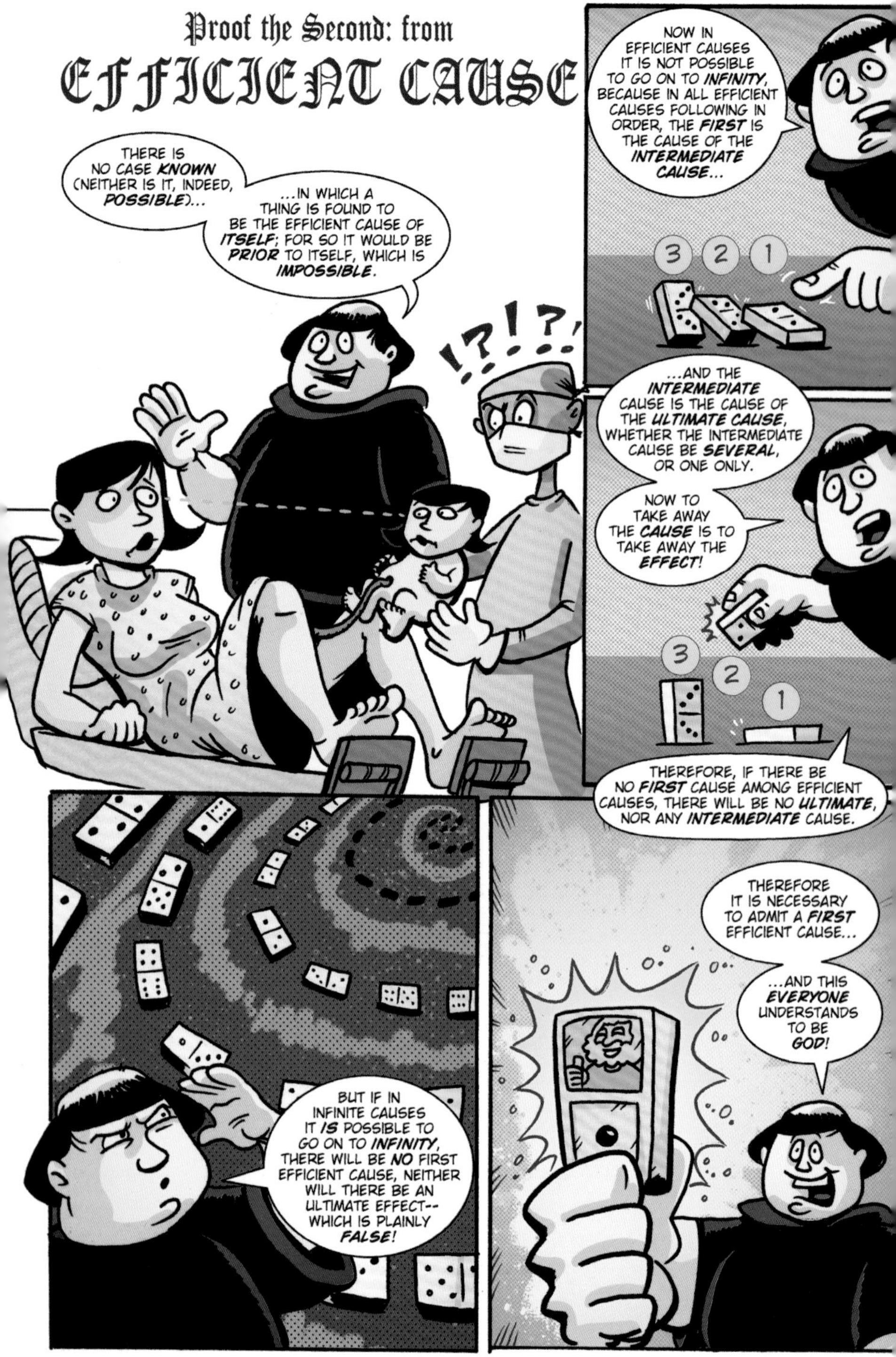
THERE IS NO CASE KNOWN (NEITHER IS IT, INDEED, POSSIBLE)...
...IN WHICH A THING IS FOUND TO BE THE EFFICIENT CAUSE OF ITSELF; FOR SO IT WOULD BE PRIOR TO ITSELF, WHICH IS IMPOSSIBLE.
!?!?!
NOW IN EFFICIENT CAUSES IT IS NOT POSSIBLE TO GO ON TO INFINITY, BECAUSE IN ALL EFFICIENT CAUSES FOLLOWING IN ORDER, THE FIRST IS THE CAUSE OF THE INTERMEDIATE CAUSE...
3 2 1
...AND THE INTERMEDIATE CAUSE IS THE CAUSE OF THE ULTIMATE CAUSE, WHETHER THE INTERMEDIATE CAUSE BE SEVERAL, OR ONE ONLY.
NOW TO TAKE AWAY THE CAUSE IS TO TAKE AWAY THE EFFECT!
3 2 1
THEREFORE, IF THERE BE NO FIRST CAUSE AMONG EFFICIENT CAUSES, THERE WILL BE NO ULTIMATE, NOR ANY INTERMEDIATE CAUSE.
BUT IF IN INFINITE CAUSES IT IS POSSIBLE TO GO ON TO INFINITY, THERE WILL BE NO FIRST EFFICIENT CAUSE, NEITHER WILL THERE BE AN ULTIMATE EFFECT--WHICH IS PLAINLY FALSE!
THEREFORE IT IS NECESSARY TO ADMIT A FIRST EFFICIENT CAUSE...
...AND THIS EVERYONE UNDERSTANDS TO BE GOD!

Proof the Third: from NECESSARY vs. POSSIBLE BEING

WE FIND IN NATURE THINGS THAT ARE POSSIBLE TO *BE* AND *NOT* TO BE.

to be

not to be

BUT IT IS *IMPOSSIBLE* FOR THESE *ALWAYS* TO EXIST, FOR THAT WHICH IS *POSSIBLE* NOT TO BE AT SOME TIME *IS NOT*.

BRING IT ON! I CANNOT NOT BE!!

delusional bunny

THEREFORE, IF *EVERYTHING* IS POSSIBLE *NOT TO BE*, THEN AT ONE TIME THERE COULD HAVE BEEN *NOTHING* IN EXISTENCE!

IF THIS WERE *TRUE*, EVEN *NOW* THERE WOULD BE *NOTHING* IN EXISTENCE, BECAUSE THAT WHICH DOES *NOT* EXIST ONLY *BEGINS* TO EXIST BY SOMETHING *ALREADY EXISTING.*

WE CANNOT *BUT* POSTULATE THE EXISTENCE OF SOME BEING HAVING OF *ITSELF* ITS OWN NECESSITY, AND NOT RECEIVING IT FROM *ANOTHER*, BUT RATHER CAUSING IN OTHERS *THEIR* NECESSITY!

THIS *ALL* MEN SPEAK OF AS *GOD!*

THEREFORE, SINCE THINGS *DO* NOW EXIST, NOT *ALL* BEINGS ARE MERELY *POSSIBLE!*

poit!

THERE *MUST* EXIST SOMETHING OF WHICH IS *NECESSARY.*

Proof the Fourth: from the
DEGREES OF PERFECTION

AMONG BEINGS THERE ARE SOME *MORE* AND SOME *LESS* GOOD, TRUE, NOBLE, AND THE LIKE.

BUT "MORE" AND "LESS" ARE PREDICATED OF DIFFERENT THINGS, ACCORDING AS THEY RESEMBLE IN THEIR DIFFERENT WAYS SOMETHING WHICH IS THE *MAXIMUM...*

...AS A THING SAID TO BE *HOTTER* ACCORDING AS IT MORE NEARLY RESEMBLES THAT WHICH IS *HOTTEST...*

...SO THAT THERE IS SOMETHING WHICH *IS* TRUEST, SOMETHING BEST, SOMETHING NOBLEST...

HOT   **NOT HOT**

...AND, CONSEQUENTLY, THERE *IS* SOMETHING WHICH IS UTTERMOST BEING...

...AS *FIRE*, WHICH IS THE MAXIMUM OF *HEAT*, IS THE CAUSE OF *ALL HOT THINGS*.

THEREFORE THERE MUST *ALSO* BE SOMETHING WHICH IS TO *ALL* BEINGS THE CAUSE OF THEIR BEING, GOODNESS, AND EVERY OTHER *PERFECTION*...

...AND *THIS* WE CALL GOD!

114

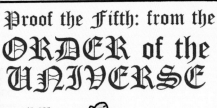

Proof the Fifth: from the ORDER of the UNIVERSE

WE SEE THAT THINGS WHICH LACK *INTELLIGENCE*--

ER...

NO...

WE MEAN *NATURAL BODIES*...

...ACT FOR AN *END*, AND THIS IS EVIDENT FROM THEIR ACTING ALWAYS, OR *NEARLY* ALWAYS, IN THE *SAME WAY*, SO AS TO OBTAIN THE *BEST RESULT*.

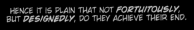

HENCE IT IS PLAIN THAT NOT *FORTUITOUSLY*, BUT *DESIGNEDLY*, DO THEY ACHIEVE THEIR END.

NOW WHATEVER LACKS INTELLIGENCE CANNOT *MOVE* TOWARDS AN END, UNLESS IT BE *DIRECTED* BY SOME BEING ENDOWED *WITH* KNOWLEDGE AND INTELLIGENCE...

...THEREFORE, *SOME* INTELLIGENT BEING EXISTS BY WHOM *ALL* NATURAL THINGS ARE DIRECTED TO THEIR END, AND *THIS* BEING WE CALL...

I @#$%&*! *HATE TRAILER PARKS!!*

...ER...YOU KNOW...

REPLY OBJ.: AS *AUGUSTINE* SAYS:

"*SINCE GOD IS THE HIGHEST GOOD*, HE WOULD NOT ALLOW *ANY EVIL* TO EXIST IN HIS WORKS...

...UNLESS HIS *OMNIPOTENCE* AND *GOODNESS* WERE SUCH AS TO BRING GOOD EVEN OUT OF *EVIL!*"

AAAHHHH! NO MORE! YOU WIN!

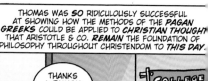

THOMAS WAS *SO* RIDICULOUSLY SUCCESSFUL AT SHOWING HOW THE METHODS OF THE *PAGAN GREEKS* COULD BE APPLIED TO *CHRISTIAN THOUGHT* THAT ARISTOTLE & CO. *REMAIN* THE FOUNDATION OF PHILOSOPHY THROUGHOUT CHRISTENDOM TO *THIS DAY.*

THANKS A *BUNCH*, AQUINAS-DUDE!

COLLEGE

ARISTOTLE'S POETICS

THOMAS SPENT THE REMAINDER OF HIS LIFE (D. 1274) PREACHING, WRITING, AND TEACHING.

CANONIZED IN *1323*, HE IS THE PATRON SAINT OF CATHOLIC *SCHOOLS* AND *UNIVERSITIES.*

HIS REPUTATION WAS ENSURED BY HIS MOST *FAMOUS* BOOK, THE *SUMMA THEOLOGICA*, A MASSIVE TREATISE CONSIDERED BY MANY TO BE THE *GREATEST* WORK OF THEOLOGY EVER *WRITTEN.*

SUMMA THEOLOGICA

AQUINAS

BUT IN ORDER TO BE A SAINT, *MIRACLES* HAVE TO BE ATTRIBUTED TO YOU TOO. IN 1273 THREE OF AQUINAS'S BROTHER MONKS SWORE THEY SAW THE CRUCIFIX IN THE MONASTERY CHAPEL *COME TO LIFE:*

Thou hast written WELL of me Thomas; what REWARD wilt thou have?

NONE OTHER THAN *THYSELF*, LORD!

NOW HOW MANY PHILOSOPHERS CAN BOAST SUCH *GLOWING REVIEWS* BY THEIR OWN *SUBJECTS?*

About the Creators

Fred Van Lente (writer, research, lettering) is the #1 New York Times Bestselling, Harvey Award-Nominated writer of too many comics to count, including *Incredible Hercules*, *Marvel Zombies*, *Archer & Armstrong*, *Weird Detective*, *The Comic Book History of Animation*, *The Comic Book History of Comics*, *The Comic Book Story of Basketball*, and the *Action Activists* and *Action Presidents* series. He's also written two prose mystery novels, *Ten Dead Comedians* and *The Con Artist*.

Ryan Dunlavey (artist) is the artist of the *Action Activists* and *Action Presidents* series, *The Comic Book History of Animation*, *The Comic Book History of Comics*, *Dirt Candy: A Cookbook*, *Polidiocy* and the writer and artist of *Tommy Atomic*, *MO.D.O.K. Reign Delay*, and lots more, probably. He really needs a nap.

Adam Guzowski (colorist) has colored comics for IDW, Image Comics, Red 5, and Boom Studios and (according to Fred and Ryan) he totally kicks ass.

Here's what's coming in...

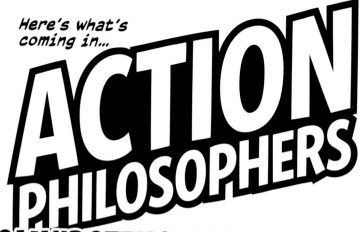

ACTION PHILOSOPHERS

"OMNIPOTENCE FOR DUMMIES"

Rene Descartes!

Baruch Spinoza!

Soren Kierkegaard!

David Hume!

Immanual Kant!

Georg Hegel!

Arthur Schopenhauer!

Niccolo Machiavelli!

Jean-Jacques Rosseau!

Mary Shelley!

and more!

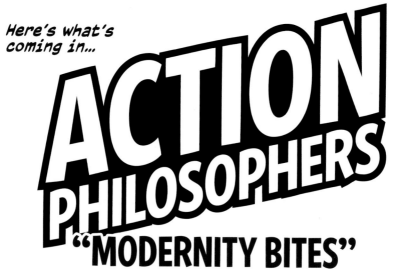

ACTION PHILOSOPHERS

"MODERNITY BITES"

Karl Marx!

John Stuart Mill!

Jean-Paul Sartre!

Friedrich Nietzsche!

Ayn Rand!

Sigmund Freud!

Carl Jung!

Joseph Campbell!

Ludwig Wittgenstein!

Jacques Derrida!

and more!

also by Fred Van Lente and Ryan Dunlavey:

Action Activists
Action Presidents: George Washington
Action Presidents: Abraham Lincoln
Action Presidents: Theodore Roosevelt
Action Presidents: John F Kennedy

also by Fred Van Lente, Ryan Dunlavey and Adam Guzowski:

The Comic Book History of Animation
The Comic Book History of Comics: Birth of a Medium
The Comic Book History of Comics: Comics For All

by Fred Van Lente:

Ten Dead Comedians
The Con Artist

by Fred Van Lente and Joe Cooper:

The Comic Book Story of Basketball

by Fred Van Lente and Crystal Skillman:

King Kirby: A Play

by Fred Van Lente and Tom Fowler:

HowToons: [Re]Ignition

by Fred Van Lente, Greg Pak and Colleen Coover:

Make Comics Like The Pros

by Amanda Cohen and Ryan Dunlavey:

Dirt Candy: A Cookbook

adapted from this book by Crystal Skillman:

Action Philosophers: The Play

find us on the internet!

fredvanlente.com
ryandunlavey.com
eviltwincomics.com